MW01698960

Shirley Fenton Huie was born in western New South Wales to a country doctor who always wanted to be a sailor. As a consequence she was surrounded from early childhood by books of adventure in distant lands as her landlocked father indulged his passion for the exotic. Shirley Fenton Huie became the adventurer her father had always wanted to be. Her passion for travel and marriage to a helicopter pilot took her all over the world, from Columbia and Honduras, to the United States, New Zealand, South Korea, Indonesia and Vanuatu, and finally to Sydney for her children's education. Today Shirley Fenton Huie works as a freelance writer for publications such as *The Australian*, *Pacific Islands Monthly*, *Vogue*, *Craft Australia* and *Nature & Health*. She has also written scripts for ABC television.

S. Loder

AND THE SECOND PRIZE IS...

ACROSS AUSTRALIA BY BUS

SHIRLEY FENTON HUIE

Collins Publishers Australia

COLLINS PUBLISHERS AUSTRALIA
First published in 1989 by William Collins Pty Ltd,
55 Clarence Street, Sydney NSW 2000

National Library of Australia
Cataloguing-in-Publication data:

Huie, Shirley Fenton.
And the second prize is . . . Across Australia by bus.

ISBN 0 7322 2527 2.
1. Bus travel — Australia. 2. Australia — Description and travel — 1976- . I. Title.
919.4'0463

Typeset in Cheltenham Light by Savage Type Pty Ltd, Brisbane
Printed by The Book Printer, Melbourne

Acknowledgements: The author wishes to thank Magabala Books for permission to reproduce the extracts from *Mayi* on page 100 and Roy Walker for permission to reproduce 'Graceful Native Girl' and the extract from 'Spinning Yarns' on page 93.

Cover photograph: The Olgas, Northern Territory, courtesy of the Australian Tourist Commission.

For Dennis
who urged me to go

CONTENTS

A 16 000-KILOMETRE JOURNEY

INTRODUCTION

Outback Australia, from 9000 metres, looks like another planet. Flying in from Asia or Europe the Western Australian coastline appears below and then the great nothingness begins. For hours, at near the speed of sound, the flight path traverses a landscape that is red, empty and forbidding.

On homecoming journeys as an expatriate, this was my perception. The barren land below and the Red Centre was the great barrier that separates most Australians from the rest of the world.

And now I am to enter this no-man's-land, travel across it at ground level, sleep on it, touch it and discover its reality. The scale of my decision brings on shivers of apprehension. What if it is unbearable? What if I hate it? Can I afford to fly back? The doubts flood in and I wonder if I've made a silly decision. But the bookings have been finalised and to withdraw would be cowardly.

The journey begins.

1

COUNTRY TOWNS, A MISLAID PASSENGER AND THE SILVER CITY

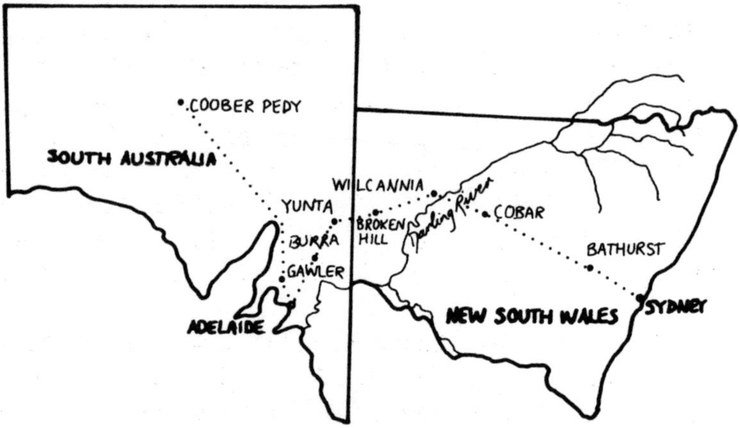

COOBER PEDY
SOUTH AUSTRALIA
WILCANNIA
YUNTA
BROKEN HILL
BURRA
GAWLER
ADELAIDE
Darling River
COBAR
BATHURST
SYDNEY
NEW SOUTH WALES

Travelling is not necessarily being on holiday. It may not even be pleasant or comfortable, but it is always the serious business of exploration and discovery.

I am about to set off on a journey that came to me by chance. For years I had hoped to meet someone travelling around Australia in a Landrover who would invite me to join. It never happened, but then, at a Christmas party, I won a prize — not the first prize, which was a trip to London, but four weeks' worth of Aussiepass with Ansett Trailways. Oh, dear! Sounded extremely uncomfortable and unexciting, but yet, the geography was right. I toyed with the offer for eight months hoping my Landrovered adventurer would appear, but no luck. As the expiry date loomed closer I knew it was now or never and threw myself into gear. I confirmed my ticket and now here I am at the beginning of a journey of over 16 000 kilometres that will take me through temperature ranges of 0°C to 50°C and landscapes of deserts, mountains and wilderness.

Departure time is 10.00 p.m. and I check in early to be sure of a good seat. A girl from the Ansett office tells me the best seat is four from the front on the left-hand side so, tendering my virginal Aussiepass, I secure this optimum place. A good start. As well as my soft zip bag and my camera bag I also carry a half-moon blow-up pillow and a full-size pillow stuffed into a string bag. The latter becomes my dearly beloved companion as the trip progresses and one of my best baggage decisions. I'm wearing ski-pants, skivvy, sneakers, a soft jacket and socks.

We leave dead on time and I wave good-bye to loved ones who anxiously assure me they will send a rescue expedition whenever I need it. Four weeks on a bus! You must be joking! But I'm not, and as we move out of the Oxford Street terminal I look back only once. I'm off into the dark night on a very real adventure.

Target points for my journey are Broken Hill, Coober Pedy, Ayers Rock and Alice Springs, Darwin and Kakadu,

Kununurra, Broome, North West Shelf, Shark Bay, Kalgoorlie and the Nullarbor. All on public transport — the scheduled coach lines serving the people of the Outback.

On the east coast of Australia we have managed to tame the rim of this alien land — alien to us — and lace it over with cities, freeways and forests of foreign trees that shed their leaves and so remind us of our origins in faraway Europe. But in the Outback, the Top End and the Kimberleys this is not so. The landscape gives nothing to remind us of our past. It is not alien. We are. It is red and rocky and forested with feathery trees daintily standing apart from one another like ballet dancers. Trees and bushes do not crowd each other but conserve the landscape. Water is scarce so each plant gives *Lebensraum* to its neighbours. Trees of palest apple-green and grey, rounded hummocks of spinifex . . . but that is yet to come. Now my journey has just begun and we are hurtling through the still known landscapes of Bathurst, Orange and Dubbo. There is a video, *Breakdance.* I'm still safe and can always fly back if it's too awful.

Country towns look mysterious at night. They are all brightly lit but there are no people. We stop at a cafe, the Acropolis, for supper and, as ever in country towns, it is run by Greeks. In my day, cafes were called the Paragon or Peters and were a far cry from this Acropolis, a fairyland of chandeliers, red velvet seats and autumn-toned carpet. The Peters cafes I remember had linoleum on the floor, palms in pots, bright ceiling lights and a long counter behind which were hidden ice creams and chocolates in the ice chest.

Is this the same Bathurst an earlier traveller, Charles Darwin, came to on horseback in 1836? His impressions as he rode into Bathurst are recorded in *The Voyage of a Naturalist Round the World in HMS Beagle:*

> In the afternoon we came in view of the downs of Bathurst. These undulating but nearly smooth plains are very remarkable in this

> country from being absolutely destitute of trees . . . we reached the township seated in the middle of what may be called either a very broad valley or a narrow plain. I was told in Sydney not to form too bad an opinion of Australia from the roadside nor too good a one from Bathurst. The secret of its growing prosperity is that the brown pasture which appears to the stranger's eye so wretched is excellent for sheep grazing. The town stands at a height of 2200 feet above the sea on the banks of the Macquarie; this is one of the rivers flowing into the vast and scarcely known interior . . . to my surprise I found it a mere chain of ponds, separated from each other by spaces almost dry. Scanty as the supply of water is throughout this district, it becomes still scantier further inland.

Darwin's guess as to conditions 'further inland' was to prove accurate. Man's ingenuity in overcoming the water problem, however, was something beyond his imagining and a revelation to me, first at Broken Hill and later at the Ord and at Kalgoorlie.

My half-moon blow-up pillow is a great aid to sleep; consequently I miss Narromine, Nyngan and Cobar. Dawn breaks and we are in the Outback. At Emmdale the young Japanese couple who joined the coach at Leura have a problem. The boy went to sleep and the girl was left behind at Cobar. The boy asks the driver to go back for her as she has no money. Return is impossible of course but the driver is solicitous. He makes a phone call from the little roadhouse and we move on. Kangaroos! In outback New South Wales the landscape is yellow, purple and dark apple-green, low scrub against a grey earth. Turpentine and wattle with their yellow blossoms and everywhere the rich purple wash of Salvation Jane, otherwise known as Patterson's Curse.

The gentle name for this ubiquitous plant is for its life-saving properties as stock feed in drought conditions and the cursed appellation for the fact that, even though the cattle and sheep find it sweet and pleasant to eat, it forms flour balls in their intestines if eaten in too great a quantity and eventually the beasts die.

We now pass masses of pom-pom daisies and some low olive-coloured scrubby trees that could be saltbush. I'll have to ask someone. The soil is now beginning to change from grey to red. Flocks of galahs, grey, white and pink rise like star bursts against the flat blue sky. Tiny white daisies spread out like a carpet. Salvation Jane is now a border to the road and the yellow turpentine flowers burn like flame in the early morning sun. The terrain is rocky and the road is excellent. How can we afford such marvellous roads? High concrete viaducts of excellent structure and durability take us across the flood plains before Wilcannia.

At a quarter to eight we cross the Darling River and pull in to Wilcannia. The Japanese girl arrives while we are having breakfast. She hitchhiked in a yellow car and tells us, 'My boyfriend is a stoopid. He should know I get off bus.'

The bus driver should know also. He is supposed to count the passengers every time the bus stops.

Wilcannia is where the first Resch's beer was brewed. Edmund Resch, a German who migrated before the First World War, settled in the outback town and sold lemonade door to door from a wheelbarrow. He later moved into brewing beer and founded the great brewing empire that bears his name.

Wilcannia is dying. In spite of the excellent road which passes through, it has only the local farmers to depend on and as things are not going well for them nowadays all the young people leave. The big country stores and hotels echoing memories of a prosperous past are closed up and shuttered. It is empty. There are no people to be seen except for little groups of Aborigines sitting under the pepper trees.

Back in the bus the driver tells us there is no scenery worth looking at from here to Broken Hill so we look instead at the video, *Top Gun*.

There is scenery, however; this time seas of swaying yellow soursobs locked about the base with low clumps of saltbush. And now the grey, purposeful pipeline bringing water from Menindee to Broken Hill slips alongside and keeps us company the rest of the way.

Morning tea time brings us into Silver City and the first traffic lights we've seen since Dubbo. The streets are named for the chemicals and minerals of the great mine: Argent Street, Chloride Street, Bromide Street, Sulphide Street, Iodine Street, names given with respect and in honour of the minerals which provided the livelihood of workers and management in this tough outback town.

Tourism is booming in Broken Hill. The city has thirteen art galleries including Pro Hart's and Jack Absalom's. There are seven art and craft shops, four museums and an Afghan mosque. Tours of the mines and visits to nearby ghost towns are on the busy daily agenda of the tour companies. Broken Hill is also a major base for both the School of the Air and the Royal Doctor Flying Service. Mining activities may be coming to a close but the people are staying on and leading the Outback in tourist development.

An elderly male passenger who went to the pub during our stopover has to be found before we can leave. POB's are carefully counted this time after the slip-up over the Japanese girl. There are more generic street names as we pull out of town: Cobalt, Beryl, Chrystal, Blende, Wolfram, Mica, Oxide, etc. These are the daughters of Broken Hill, their names perpetuated forever on street corners.

We are now travelling parallel to the Indian-Pacific Railway and along the track for miles and miles are stacked great piles of concrete sleepers, in readiness to replace the current wooden ones. As with the great roads we now begin to see where the tax money goes. It is truly surprising that the deeper one penetrates the Outback the better the roads become. Quite the reverse of the past when the dusty corrugated tracks that took you westward were bone-shattering and axle-wrenching to vehicles not specifically built for rough conditions. This highway is as smooth as glass with culverts neatly concreted, lay-offs at appropriate distances and excellent directional signposts. It would be hard to get lost here unless you left the main road and disregarded signs.

Lunch in Yunta at 'Dings', who 'Has Everything'. Then on past Terowie, a ghost town of stone houses, many of them falling apart stone by stone. What disaster struck here? Did the well dry up or were they overrun by Patterson's Curse. No one on the bus knows.

On down the rich, beautiful and expansive Burra Valley fully sown in cereal crops and prosperous with stone farm-houses. Through charming colonial Gawler and finally Adelaide at 4.00 p.m.

At this point I decide that instead of staying overnight in Adelaide I will carry on to Coober Pedy making the first lap of my journey 36 hours and a distance of 2000 kilometres. A shower in the terminal is not the easiest I've ever had. The stall is small with nowhere to put possessions. The shower rose sprays out in all directions so I manage to wet most of my things with the fine mist. But it is at least good to feel fresh again and ready for a second night sleeping on the bus. As the weeks pass I learn how to get enough sleep. The secret is to drop off whenever you feel drowsy and not wait for the usual sleeping time during the night. With a double seat it's possible to curl into a foetal position, head to the aisle and feet hard against the window wall. Jumpsuits and socks are the best gear as the interior of the bus is always cool even in the hottest latitudes. A good pillow is essential and the half-moon blow-ups are great for day-time napping. Most of the food in the roadhouses is pretty awful — Chiko rolls, pies and pasties — so I always keep a good supply of dried fruit, nuts and fruit juice to sustain life. Straws are essential when you drink on buses which travel at somewhere between 110 and 120 kilometres per hour. They pass most of the traffic on the road and overtaking a four-trailer road train is quite a thrill. It seems you will never get past but as the road stretches ahead some 100 kilometres in a straight line it's easy to see if there is anything coming.

Drivers of overland coaches in the Outback are all highly experienced, many of them having driven road trains themselves, and quite a number have driven twenty years for Ansett. Without exception they are enthusiastic about their job and the Outback and do their best to impart this to the passengers. The first thing they do is introduce themselves:

'My name is Mike and I will be going through to Coober Pedy with you where you will get a new driver. Behind the coach you will have noticed that we are towing an Australia Post trailer. This is a service we provide to the people of the Outback. We will soon be calling in to a fruit and vegetable shop on the outskirts of Adelaide to pick up some fresh fruit for the people out there. I suggest that if you like fruit yourself then stock up on it here as it comes very expensive the further north you get. The journey to Coober Pedy will take us nine hours and we'll have a brief stop at Port Augusta along the way so you can get a cup of tea. The toilet is situated at the back of the coach. Do not put anything into it except the paper provided [*sic!*]. And always lock the door, otherwise when the bus comes to a sudden halt to avoid a kangaroo or a camel you will find yourself propelled down the aisle and probably end up in my lap. Now that's enough to make you lock the door if anything is! The seats are aircraft recliners. Before you put them into recline please alert the passenger behind you who may be bending down to tie up his shoelaces and suddenly find himself clamped into a head lock and possibly suffering a broken neck. Please also put your waste paper and rubbish into the bags provided. It may be of interest to hear that when we carry a bus load of Japanese tourists it's the only time we don't have to clean the bus afterwards. They leave the bus exactly as they entered it. Clean. Now if you all settle back we'll see what sort of a movie we can put on for you.'

At the front of the bus, high above the windscreen, is the video screen, clearly visible to all. Sound comes from speakers above each seat in the control panel for reading lights and air conditioners. The videos are very popular with the passengers and in my four weeks I see a total of sixteen videos with only one repeat.

We stop at Virginia to buy fruit and watch Mike load everything from carrots and potatoes and greens to oranges, apples and bananas into the trailer for the Outback.

A pretty Aboriginal woman with four small children is in the seat across the aisle from me. She tells me she is returning to her own country east of Alice Springs after a holiday in Adelaide. The children are quiet as mice. Later she puts two to bed side by side on a spare seat in front and the other two across her lap. All rugged up with pillows and blankets they watch the video with wide, shining eyes.

After midnight we stop at Pimba but no one gets off. This is where you de-bus for the Woomera Rocket Range. No anti-nuke protestors on board this time. Then on through Glendambo, which I blissfully miss and finally come to a halt in Coober Pedy, my first destination.

2

COOBER PEDY, DUGOUTS AND NOODLING

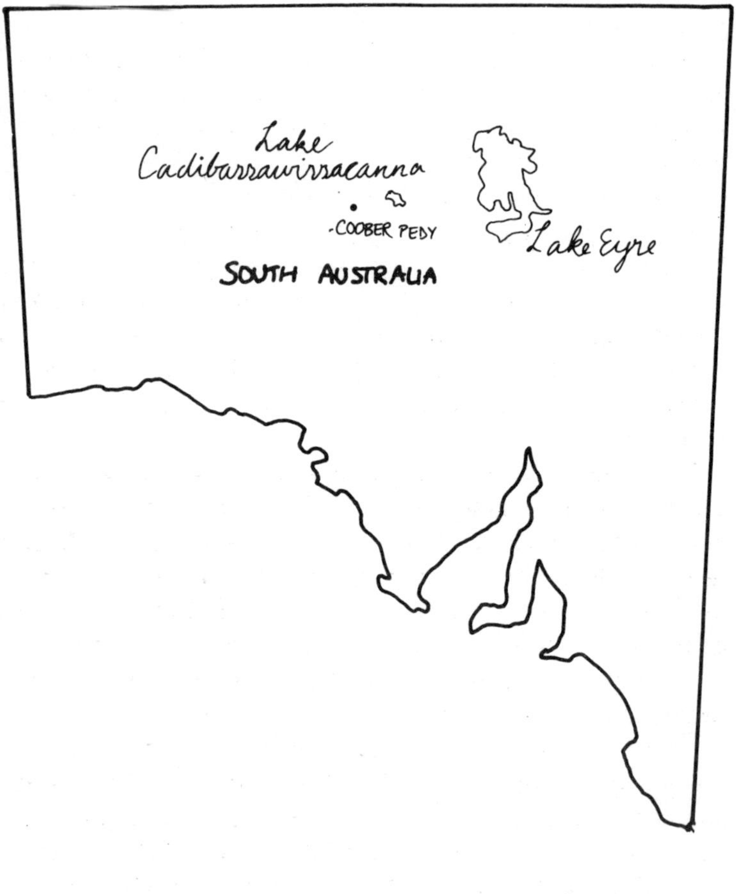
Lake
Cadibarrawirracanna
COOBER PEDY
Lake Eyre
SOUTH AUSTRALIA

At 5.00 a.m. this famous opal town is invisible, because of the darkness and because most of it is underground. Not just the miners working at the rock face but the houses and hotels and even the youth hostel. The bus driver Mike takes pity on me and offers coffee and company until daylight. He is being relieved here by a new driver.

After the coffee he offers me a beer which I drink happily. The first time I've been in to that at 5.00 a.m. He talks a lot, mainly about the people he carries and says his best passengers are the Japanese:

'They are always very friendly. I had a group come down from Alice Springs last year. Two of them adopted me as their father and sent me back pictures from Japan. One still writes to me and tells me what she's doing. They are very friendly people. And very courteous. Adelaide is a sister city to Penang in Malaysia but also to Hiji on Kyushu. I believe it is also sister city to Christchurch in New Zealand and a city in Texas.'

Mike had ten years on the trucks before he joined Pioneer, driving anywhere between Adelaide and Mackay in Queensland. The only accident he ever had was when his brakes failed at the Victoria Pass on the Blue Mountains. He threw the gears into reverse and took the cliff face, rather than risk going over the side and down some several hundred metres. Pioneer has a virtually accident-free record over the last twenty-five years (touch wood).

'Kangaroos can do a lot of damage. I had a six-foot-six one that just got me at the right time. Snapped the bull-bar in half and came right into the front of the coach. Woke up all my passengers! That was on this road before it was sealed, round about Kingoonya. Cattle are a problem further north. You've got to be careful with them. They can do a lot of damage when you are travelling at up to 100 kilometres an hour.

'Over in the west it's nothing to see twenty or thirty camels wandering across the road. We've got about 50 000 wild ones in Australia. Flying insects are a big problem on the windscreen. It's nothing to stop two or three times during a journey and clean them off so you can see.'

The country is so dry and treeless that I ask him if dust storms are a problem.

'We get them here. Go down to the bookshop in Coober Pedy. He's got a photo of a dust storm and it looks just like a wave in the sea. It was 60 to 70 feet high and engulfed the town like a tidal wave. Last year there was a big one which demolished a third of the town. That's why a lot of people are going back underground. They had come up but they are going down again.'

People went below ground because of the harshness of the climate and its temperatures of up to 57°C. Living underground they get natural ventilation by drilling holes in the roof which causes a wind tunnel, allowing the wind to come through naturally. Below ground the temperature never gets above 25°C.

'About five years ago, when the road was dirt, I used to drive to here and then go right on to Alice Springs. We'd pick up vegetables and fruit like we did this time and drop them off as we went along. One drop was at Widna between here and Marla Bore. We'd turn off the highway, over the creek, and go right up to the house, unload the veggies and even help them to pack everything away. The young girl there had a pet horse and that horse knew exactly which bin the fruit was in. If we weren't quick enough he'd come right up and lean against the door and wouldn't budge until we gave him some carrots. The girl really liked animals and used to keep joeys when the mother had died. She'd bring them down to the coach and let everyone pet them. But now that the road's sealed all the way to Darwin, you don't get that sort of thing any more. It's just another run. On the dirt road the scheduled time from Adelaide to Alice Springs was 29 hours but it could take up to a week. You'd break down, get bogged, or things would fall off the coach and you'd have passengers sleeping all over the place. Or the wet season would come in early and you'd get stuck and they'd fly in provisions for you until you could get out.'

It is daylight now so I set off to explore this town. Visible buildings are the Opal Motel, half a dozen shops related to opal buying, post office, supermarket but not much else. Knowing Coober Pedy's reputation for temperatures in the 40s and 50s I am glad it is early morning and still pleasantly cool.

Underground dwellings are called 'dugouts' and there are several along the main road offering budget-style accommodation and also a very swank-looking hotel still under construction. Reception is above ground and there are differing prices for both topsides and below ground, the latter being higher. Dugouts are not so much directly underground as dug out of low hills. The youth hostel is a dugout run by June Radeka. More about her later.

The name 'Coober Pedy' comes from the Aboriginal words, *kupa piti* meaning 'white man down a hole'. The word 'opal' was first used by the Romans who believed the gemstone came from India where the locals called it *upala.* Opals were mined in Mexico and Hungary but none of these displayed the brilliant fire that was present in the Australian opal. By 1905 opals had already been discovered in Angaston, White Cliffs, Opalton and Lightning Ridge. Then, in 1915, a young lad called Willie Hutchison, prospecting for gold with his dad, found opal on the surface and the opal rush was on. Many diggers, back from the trenches in France, came to try their luck and were later followed by out-of-work Italians from the mica mines in Alice Springs. Nowadays 80 per cent of the world's opals come from the South Australian fields and are worked by miners from forty-five different countries.

Sadly the Hutchisons had no part in the developing bonanza. They moved on to go droving in Queensland and young Willie was drowned in a creek. All that remains is Hutchison Street named in honour of his lucky find. It is Coober Pedy's main thoroughfare.

Over 2000 people of different nationalities live in the town which at first sight gives the appearance of a giant junk yard. Dumped machinery lies everywhere but of course it is invisible to the inhabitants living below ground in their dugouts. A layer of fine dust covers everything in town, even down in the dugouts. Seeping through glass-fronted display cases, it covers all in a thin grey veil. It's the first time I've seen apples and oranges through a web of grey in a supermarket.

Down the road, totally underground, is St Peter and St Paul's Catholic Church, and I learn that the Anglican Catacomb Church is likewise a dugout. The communion table is a miner's winch and beneath it hangs the traditional bucket.

It's now getting on for 8.00 a.m. and people are beginning to emerge and shake the dust from their eyes. Thanks to Ansett Trailways I am booked 'in' at the Opal Motel and also receive a courtesy invitation to join a local bus tour.

Paul Olsen, a young man who came here on a visit and stayed on like so many others, is our driver and guide. He explains that opal mining appeals to many people because the gems are not taxed until they are processed. Raw opal sells from several dollars an ounce, up to 8000 dollars for high grade material. Chinese are the main opal buyers. If things are slow, miners' wives and children can go out to the mullock or waste dumps and make extra money by fossicking around. This is called 'noodling' and it can keep the family in 'tucker money' until the miner has better luck. The Stuart Ranges, where the opals are found, were named after the explorer, John McDouall Stuart, who passed through the area in the 1850s.

To discover if a hill is inhabited, Paul explained that first you look for a water tank standing alone and then for a tall ventilation shaft, like a periscope, alongside. Most dugouts are freehold title and some are quite luxurious with swimming pools on top and maybe two storeys below. Some have up to six ventilator shafts and from these you can judge the size of the dwelling below. A ten-room dugout could sell for

$60 000 or more. There is now a public piped water system of desalinated bore water for the town, so many of the old tanks are empty and no longer needed. Paul says you often see them rolling round the town on windy days.

Many of the dugouts were once mines but there is no mining in the town these days for safety reasons. If you should desire to extend your dugout by digging an extra room, you could be lucky and find an opal bearing seam in the wall. This would pay for your extensions but of course you wouldn't say where the opal came from.

Tunnelling machines, which are a Coober Pedy invention, make a drive a metre wide and the height of a man. Charges are about $45 per metre so it would cost $10 000 to dig a four-room dugout.

Before going mining you must obtain a Precious Stone Prospector's Permit which costs $27 and is valid for twelve months. With the permit comes four small plastic plates with your number on them and these you attach to special pegs bought from the hardware shop. Next you look for a claim either in an old field or on virgin ground, take compass bearings to make sure it is 50 metres square and find the nearest Mines Reference Peg. These are usually painted a fluorescent colour and, depending on the location of the field, are marked with specific letters and numbers. They are laid out on a grid pattern, about 200 metres apart, around each of the fields. Having found the peg you now take further measurements and a compass bearing. All this information is then taken to the local Mines Department which marks it on its map as your registered claim. And that's not all, as Paul continues:

'Records are kept to check on how much work a miner does in a week as a minimum of twenty hours is required in order to keep a claim. If these hours worked cannot be shown the department can come and pull the pegs up. Someone else could be mining there instead of you. Mining must begin within fourteen days of the claim being lodged.'

There are no big company leases in Coober Pedy. Each

claim belongs to a single miner but some do go into partnership when they have adjoining claims. All members of a family can put in claims — wives, children and girlfriends; the minimum age is sixteen.

Opals found on the surface are called 'floaters' and this was what the Hutchisons found in 1915. Over many thousands of years erosion has exposed seams leaving material on the slopes and escarpments. Floaters can still be found 10 kilometres east of the town but these have curiosity value only, being badly sunbleached and cracked.

The Department of Mines' handbook defines opals as follows:

> All precious opal in South Australia occurs in rocks affected by weathering during the Tertiary Period (1.8 to 70 million years ago). The weathering process broke down minerals of the country rock to produce kaolin the soluble silica. It also created cavities in the rock by dissolving out soluble minerals and fossil shells. These cavities, together with faults and fractures in the rock, provided pathways for underground water containing the soluble silica. Periodic lowering of the water table, possibly caused by changes in climate, carried silica-rich solutions downwards to deposit opal in the rock cavities.

Precious opal still contains 6–10 per cent water.

In the early days the most sophisticated gear was the hand winch or windlass like the one I saw used as an altar in the Catacomb Church. Picks and shovels were the main tools and explosives were for the lucky ones. Once a shaft is dug the sides are inspected for opal-bearing seams and if things look favourable explosive charges are used to enlarge the area, thus giving room to swing a pick. These areas are called 'ballrooms'.

As Paul tells it: 'You drill holes a metre into the wall with an electrical pneumatic drill well about the "level" where the opal is as you don't want the opal to come out looking like sugar. The "jelly", rolled up in paper and called a sausage, is stuck in the holes and set off with gunpowder fuses and detonators. You light them in sequence, starting with the middle one. Middle, top, two sides, middle top and two sides, and then run like hell!'

The miner cannot return for about five hours, and sometimes longer in hot weather, because the explosives create poisonous fumes. The explosive used is called 'ampho' or 'nitro' and is a mixture of ammonium nitrate fertiliser mixed with small amounts of fuel oil. A powerful spotlight is used after the blast and if a flash of colour is seen the seam is dug out by hand.

Miners also listen. When there is a glassy sound, like metal on glass, that is a sure sign that opal has been hit. Opal can also be exposed in other forms, usually potch, as shells, pippi shells, mussels, snails, plant sections, vertebrae of fish and even parts of dinosaurs. Potch is milky white and does not show any play of colours.

The tour of the mine now being over, Paul invites us to spend half an hour noodling on the mullock dumps and to my great surprise and joy I find at least half a dozen lumps of rock with blue-grey opal showing clearly. Splendid souvenirs of an enthralling day.

Mike had suggested I talk to June Radeka who with her husband Ivan runs the Radeka Dugout Motel. As well as motel accommodation, there is a youth hostel in the lowest level of their dugout.

June is very warm and welcoming and as we sip tea in the cool of her underground reception area, a German backpacker pops his head round the door.

'Iss very nice your underground. I look round little bit, then I come back.'

Everyone comes back to June Radeka. Her dugout and the welcome she gives are so genuine, how could anyone resist? We talk for a while and then the German returns and June asks Ivan to take him down to the level on which youth hostel accommodation is located.

As I heard in the morning it is a pleasant 25°C underground and June shows me the vents which provide air circulation. In the old days, she says, they were built with a bend in them to prevent snakes from sliding down into the dugout.

'Yes,' she says, in answer to my startled look, 'they were a problem. In the early days there was no electricity, no generators, so people used carbide lamps or candles, kerosene refrigerators and hurricane lamps. Lighting was very poor and there were few women here. They used the hand windlass and there were no hydraulic lights so everything was done by pulleys. Then generators were brought in and that's what moved the snakes out. They don't like vibrating surfaces. We used to have coral snakes, green snakes, browns and coppers but now with the machinery and all the cats and dogs, snakes are no longer a problem. How did I come here? Well, we were doing goldsmithing and gemmology in Melbourne and came up here on a holiday and to get some opal set. We loved it so much that we came back again the next year and bought this dugout. Three years later when we'd finished our courses we moved up here permanently. That was in 1969. We had to bring enough water to last us a month and there was no electricity and no roads, just goat tracks. Water was only used for the most basic washing and drinking and this was only twenty years ago.

'We were very poor at the time but when the property at the back came up we decided to take a risk and buy it. It was a dugout on another part of the hill but we were able to join it up with our original dugout by tunnelling. We've now enlarged that area and made it into two family rooms with ensuite and a communal dining room and kitchen. I'll show you later on.

'It's an adventure to stay in these places, inside the rock of the earth. The youth hostel is on a lower level still, that's why we call it "The Dungeon". It has two large rooms with bunk beds, one for males and one for females.'

June tells me that as far as she has been able to ascertain there is no Aboriginal folklore related to Coober Pedy.

'This is a very terrible desert with no water. You can perish here in half a day if you are not prepared. Ranging very rarely brought Aborigines here. In the jasper fields there is some evidence that they used the stone, which is in the same family as flint and chalcedony, to make spear points but it would only have been for brief periods when they could carry enough water to survive.'

The Radekas have two sons and a daughter and I ask June what the children thought of growing up and living underground.

'Our younger son always loved it. He went to Scotland as an engineer, met a young lady and rang me saying, "I'm coming home with a Scottish girl to be married underground." It was a fabulous wedding, all underground. Then when Edward got married the young one came back from China for that too. He loves it.'

She then took me to see the youth hostel. We walk through a tunnel which leads to a flight of thirty-two steps going down. You can feel it getting cooler at each step. June indicates two different colours in the stone here, dark orange and pink. I feel the pink which is very cool. She tells me it is aluminium.

There is a lovely feeling of peace down here. June says it is because the ground has never been subjected to any kind of upheaval. The lines are all horizontal. The ground does not transmit seismic shock waves.

'In the 1950s there was a lot of out-of-date ammunition from the army to be disposed of so they took it all up to the Flinders Ranges. When they blew it up the shock waves were felt as far away as Alice Springs but nothing at all was recorded in Coober Pedy.

'In spite of the coolness there is no damp down here. Nothing rusts. There is only one problem in the hot summer when you come in from outside and your body is trying to cool you down by sweating. You can go to bed perfectly dry and wake up wet. This is from your own body mechanism and nothing to do with the cave. We've asked what to do about it and do you know what the experts said? Put heaters in! Heaters when it's 50 degrees outside!'

June operates the Mine Rescue Squad Radio. It is the emergency radio for search and rescue and has direct links to police and the hospital. When there are accidents in the field June acts as liaison between them. She explains how it works.

'Three people saw a man fall down a shaft and two of them went to his aid while the third one ran to the mine warden who happened to be working his claim. He got on his radio on emergency frequency which was picked up at Port Augusta and relayed back to me and then from me to the hospital. The whole thing only took a couple of minutes and within five minutes of the accident happening we had someone going down the shaft. The slowest part was getting someone to answer the phone at the hospital!

'There is a security problem in the mines as they are so spread out. Someone left a note at the bottom of a shaft saying, "This mine is booby trapped." The next day when they came back there was another note pinned over it. "It may or may not have been booby trapped yesterday, but it certainly is today."

'Ratting on other people's mines is called "night shifting" and it does go on. If you are onto opal you have to guard it twenty-four hours a day. But there is a certain honesty and I've never heard of anyone night shifting when someone was injured.'

Living in a desert environment June has an unusual attitude to trees.

'If you go up to the Big Winch you can see so far that it's an extraordinary experience. You have to train your eye to see the far distance by starting with the foreground and then moving your eyes further and further out. When you first get up there you really can't see as far as you are looking. It takes practice. You see so far that you realise how really puny we are. In places like Gippsland, with trees all over the place, I get a feeling of claustrophobia. We took Esther on a trip right round the coast up to Brisbane and I really got to hate trees because I couldn't see through them to places in the distance I wanted to look at. You can live without trees.'

After my shocked reaction to this extraordinary statement she goes on:

'Living underground has a very calming effect on you. In a house there is creaking and groaning all around you and the roof is rattling. But in a dugout it is always calm. I couldn't imagine living in a house again. A well-designed dugout has cool air all the time, whereas houses are just blocks of stagnant air. We live in this great flat plate that has been lying here ever since the Cretaceous Age and has never been subjected to stress.'

Just about everyone in Coober Pedy has an interesting story to tell, according to June. There's a wonderful old man who lives up at the hospital, called Leigh Robins. He came here as a boy of fourteen and carted water with a camel cart from a bore 15 kilometres away. He would hand-pump water up to tanks after first giving the clients a cupful to taste. If they didn't like the taste they could refuse. Sometimes it was so awful that it curdled milk and had a scum on the top.

The worst thing that ever happened to the Radekas was when their son fell down a shaft.

'He was just fourteen and when we got him up and over to the hospital there was no doctor but we were lucky enough to find one who was visiting. While we were waiting up there for news we could hear a voice in another room going on and on. It was an old man who had been down a shaft for a week and was badly dehydrated. He was so happy to be rescued that he couldn't stop talking. He had two nephews on the field but it was a week before they took their uncle's disappearance seriously. Apparently he went walking round the field with only a candle and when it blew out he fell 40 feet into an abandoned shaft. Luckily he got caught astride a

44-gallon drum that had wedged there. He called out and heard people calling him but it was a week before he was found!'

June plays the piano and violin and also sings and draws. Her son Edward is an opal cutter and later in the evening offers to cut my 'noodles' for me. Only one is worth it so for an hour I watch him fashion and polish it until he presents me with a pale milky tear drop with several flashes of fire and worthy of being set in a ring. I am moved by his generous dexterity and amused by his titillating statement that the next day he is going on safari to Cadibarrawirracanna. I look it up and find it is halfway to Lake Eyre on a doubtful road.

Walking back to my hotel that night I pass groups of Aborigines in mixed family groups sitting on street corners, and calling out to each other in their own language. I can hear them from my room all through the night and wonder what on earth it can mean.

Later on during my journey I buy Peter Brokensha's book, *The Pitjantjatjara and their Crafts,* and read the following paragraph which is perhaps an explanation:

> An activity involving both men and women is the time spent on communications amongst the group. During the day this involves continuous movement between the *wiltjas* [lean-to brush and bark shelters] of those in the camp but it was during the evening and occasionally just before dawn that total camp discussion was carried on. Although the *wiltjas* were laid out in a rough circle with a radius of about 25 metres these discussions were carried on sometimes for as long as two hours without the participants leaving their own hearth. The men particularly have remarkable powers of oratory, effortlessly using all the orator's skills of changes in volume, inflexion and tone as well as repetition and all this to an audience up to 25 or 30 metres away. These discussions often become most animated and even verbally violent but during my stay at least never led to violence or fighting. It would appear on the surface that this is a rather

elegant social device that enabled people to give vent to emotions and test group opinion on issues under a fabricated cloak of distance and anonymity although the voices of the actors were of course well known to each other.

3

AYERS ROCK, THE OLGAS AND A MAGICAL MEETING

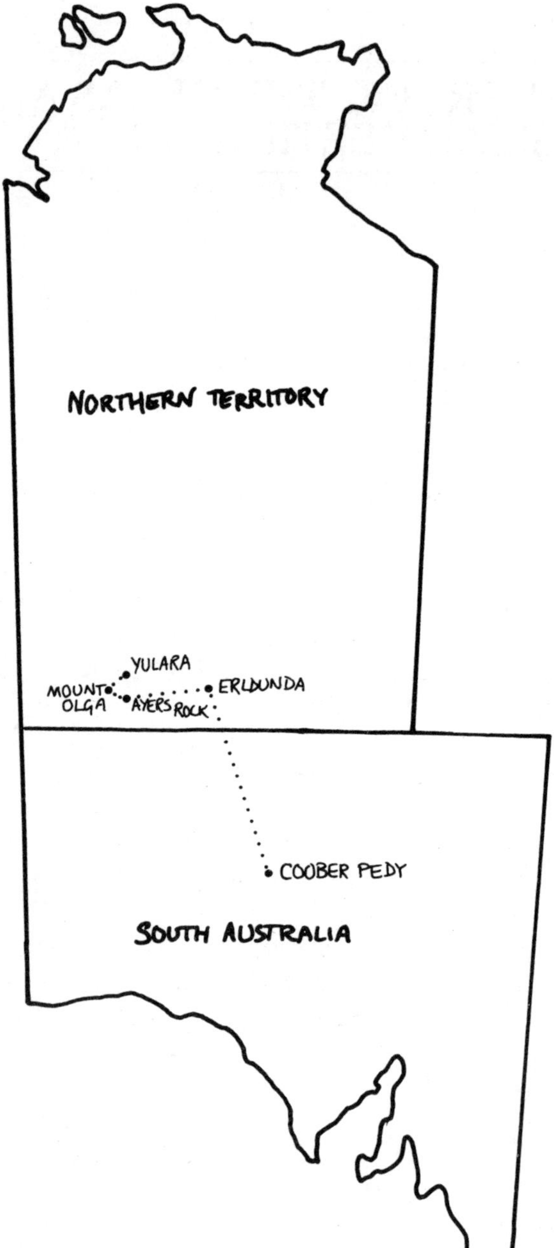
NORTHERN TERRITORY
YULARA
MOUNT OLGA
ERLDUNDA
AYERS ROCK
COOBER PEDY
SOUTH AUSTRALIA

Arriving at 5.00 a.m. means departing at 5.00 a.m. so once again I am out on the dark road waiting for the coach to take me north. Not nearly enough time in Coober Pedy as I didn't see the outlying areas, the underground potteries, the museum or Crocodile Harry's home. But my Aussiepass is ticking away and I still have many thousands of kilometres to travel in my thirty days.

Right on time the coach looms up out of the gloom and startled, bleary-eyed passengers peer out to see whoever could be joining at this godforsaken place. It's not a tea-and-pee stop so as soon as my bags are stowed away and I've found a seat, the doors slam shut and we are off north, destination Ayers Rock.

Breakfast at Marla Bore — 'Marla' coming from *malu,* Aboriginal word for kangaroo — in the best and cleanest roadhouse on the run, owned by an ex-Ansett Trailways captain who saw the necessity for a service on this long stretch of desert. It is also where the Ghan — the train from Adelaide to Alice Springs — crosses the Sturt Highway, and the turn off for both Oodnadatta and the Mintabie opal fields which have recently outstripped Coober Pedy in production.

Three hours later the roadhouse at Erldunda is frantically busy with six coaches in the parking lot. This is the turn-off point to Ayers Rock for those not wanting to carry on straight up the highway to Alice Springs. This seems a good idea, so the obliging coach captain changes my ticket and I can now take the direct route to the Rock.

The new captain is Dave and he puts *Ben Hur* on for us, to pass the time. There are lots of false alarms as we think we see Ayers Rock rising out of the red plain. But it is only Mt Connor. We arrive in Yulara at 2.00 p.m. I have travelled 1250 kilometres from Coober Pedy.

One passenger is let off at the Sheraton Hotel, an impossible dream of luxury and splendour in the desert. A beautiful young English hostess, dressed like a Hollywood cowboy, welcomes us to the resort and describes the facilities. We drive on to the Four Seasons, a less expensive but equally luxurious resort, then to the caravan park, and finally to Ayers Rock Lodge where all the backpackers and I get off. Twelve dollars a night plus extra for pillow and blanket. A bargain. I share a cabin with two English girls and a Swiss ski instructor who has just finished six months at Thredbo. The accommodation is good value with communal showers and laundries, reasonably priced canteen, lots of shady places to sit and read or write and a huge tank of rain water for drinking. Rain water is known here as 'desert champagne'.

The Swiss girl and I find we are both booked for the Olgas at 2.30 so we rush back to the entrance and just make it. Everything runs strictly to time out here. It's not like the old days when people would say, 'I'll meet you in town on Friday', and the hour was irrelevant.

Off we go, with Dave in charge. He talks most of the way and takes us to Kodak Hill, so named for its good position for taking photographs of the Olgas. Like Alice I feel like stretching myself on tiptoe and peeping over the edge of the mushroom and seeing a blue caterpillar smoking a hookah. This is Wonderland.

Dave describes how the Aborigines use spinifex to strain water. *Spinifex paradoxus* is a thick tangle of tufted spiky cane grass and placed over a container is ideal for filtering out unwanted matter. And we see trees that wear knee-high socks of thick black bark to protect them from the low brush fires that frequently sweep through the dry grass. And the seeds of many trees that germinate only in a bush fire. Repeating the old joke Dave warns us to take note of all this because 'there will be questions later'. We laugh. But in fact there are questions later, on the homeward bus, and the lucky winners are rewarded with free beer tickets.

The Aboriginal name for the Olgas is Kata Tjuta. The name 'Mount Olga' was given by the explorer Ernest Giles in 1872 on a journey that nearly took his life. Looking south from the rim of a great salt lake to which he had given the unlikely name of Amadeus, in honour of a short-time king of Spain, he saw the great tumble of rocks away to the south and immediately thought of Olga, Grand Duchess of Russia. Before moving on westwards he noted the great monolith of Uluru even further to the south but failed to give it a princely title. The naming of Uluru as Ayers Rock, a year later, was left to surveyor W. A. Gosse who honoured the land developer Sir Henry Ayers.

Like a mirage these pale pink creatures, the Olgas, loom out of the dust before our astonished eyes, their rounded minarets, giant cupolas and monstrous towers begging to enfold us in their warm and fleshlike embrace. Aborigines say they were created by dancing women, the Kunkarankakalpa. This is easy to believe for they are very female rocks. Like the school girls at Hanging Rock one feels it could be a danger to wander too long among the gullies and passes lest one should also mysteriously disappear. There is magic here. You can feel it.

We take our photos and eventually scramble back into our bus, only one of many at the Olgas at this time. Returning to Yulara along the dusty but good road — soon to be replaced by, of all things, a monorail — we are flagged down by a small group of hikers, three men and a woman. They have come out of the central pass in the Olgas, the Valley of the Winds, and as we approach I see to my great surprise that two of them, a man and a woman, are my dear friends, the Sahms, from Sydney. Their astonishment at finding me on the bus equals mine. It's more than a coincidence, it's magic! I knew they were planning a trip to the Centre but not exactly when.

Due to a mistake in the booking, they are ensconced in a super de luxe suite at the Sheraton instead of your common or garden de luxe type. We wallow in the steam bath, lounge around on the settees, try out the televisions in both the bed and sitting rooms, and finally gaze with awe at the changing sunset colours of Ayers Rock cleverly placed directly in front of the verandah. Gin and tonics from the fridge at about $6 a pop never tasted so good.

In spite of the luxurious nature of the accommodation, with room prices ranging from $155 to $300 a night, the Yulara Sheraton is surprisingly low-key, sitting as it does on the desert floor, only viewing distance from mighty Uluru. The nature of the place and setting put great demands on its architect, Philip Cox. Dealing with the problems of the shifting sand dunes and fragile plant life required all his skill and ingenuity. Giant sails, hoisted aloft on tall masts, provide shade and air circulation above the recreation areas. Startlingly white against the red earth and Nolan blue sky, they are a reminder of the explorers' tent encampments of long ago. The enormous swimming pool is the inland sea sought by dreaming travellers. Bars and restaurants are oases of cool greenery, shelters from the pitiless sun. Desalinated water comes from underground bores. Nothing is wasted; even sewage is recycled to keep the gardens fresh and green.

Guests in designer label tropical gear drift about the cool corridors, many of them Japanese and American. The one group of people who are conspicuously hidden from view in the National Park, either at the landmarks or in the hotels and camping grounds, are the traditional owners of this land, the Aborigines themselves. Their artwork and cultural totems decorate the walls and corner spaces of the hotels but the people themselves are nowhere to be seen except at the Parks and Wildlife display centre out near the Rock. Here an attempt has been made to demonstrate the type of housing they use in the form of *wiltjas* or lean-to bark and brush shelters and there are one or two old, bearded Aborigines guarding the tables of carvings for sale in the fenced-off area.

The next day our coach captain Dave gives us stern instructions on how to act around Aborigines should we chance to see any out at the Rock.

'On no account take photos of Aboriginal people. It is strictly against their custom to allow it. They also don't like being looked at so please remember that. They also have different habits of hygiene from us and regard water as a sacred liquid only to be used ceremonially or in the preparation of food. They do not use it on their bodies for washing. Consequently they smell different from us. We ask you to respect this custom and not act in any way as though you find them offensive. It is better to stay clear of them entirely.'

The consequence of all these admonitions is to leave us, the tourists, apprehensive about even glancing at Aboriginal people whenever we see them: we turn away from them and restrain our button fingers on our cameras. And so we and they become two distinct groups, moving through each other but not touching. It is as though they are anti-matter, and although vaguely visible like shadows, completely incommunicado and untouchable. Do they like to be treated as invisible? I don't know because I do exactly as ordered by my captains.

People fall off the Rock, although the number is kept *sotto voce.* There are metal plaques in memory of several who have died. Things also fall off or are blown off. Fossicking around the western side for an hour or so we collect three pairs of glasses — both sun and reading — a camera, four hats, a bag and a jacket as they come cascading down the rock towards us. Must be great pickings every day for the local inhabitants. The wind is at gale force and only the steel rope keeps the climbers from following their possessions to a sudden drop. One of the coach captains has climbed the Rock 600 times. He says there's no thrill in it now that the rope is there.

The wind is too strong today for children; they are literally lifted off their feet by the force of the wind. Aged Japanese tourists plug on relentlessly and make it to the top, ticking off another conquest.

In the evening we are taken out to Ayers Rock again, along with twenty to thirty other busloads, as well as people in Landrovers, jeeps, station wagons and sedans, to see the wonder of the changing colours of the Rock at sunset. We all line up, Kodaks at the ready to record the unfolding miracle. Disneyland has nothing on this!

I have dinner with the Sahms and we spend the free-beer tickets we won from the bus quiz. The next morning it's time to move on to Alice Springs, a surprising 480 kilometres away. We pass the turn-off to Palm Valley, a tropical oasis left stranded in a dry sunset. Here still flourish the world's most ancient palm trees, *Livistona mariae*, wondering where all the water went when the inland sea dried up. And now we cross the mighty Finke, so named by explorer McDouall Stuart in honour of a land speculator who backed his expedition. The Finke is all dust and sand, living on a memory of water yet still accredited the world's most ancient river bed.

The five-hour journey gives me an opportunity to reflect on the apparent chance encounter with my friends at Kata Tjuta.

Some people believe that the souls of the departed hang about in graveyards, their wispy eminences drifting through granite headstones, bemoaning with their filmy fellows a mutual absence of bodily form. In the presence of Uluru and Kata Tjuta in the half light of dawn and at eventide it is easy to believe in spiritual occurrences. I watched those great rocks die in their customary royal purple, crowned in deeper velvet glory. I knew that something extra special and unusual was about to occur. At the second turning of the second bend in the road leading from the park it was made manifest. Earlier on that day I had been thinking a lot about the Sahms and wondering where they were staying in Alice Springs and then there they were, walking towards me out of the chasm. Was it the web of Tjukurpa?

I believe so. 'Tjukurpa' is a word of the Anangu people, traditional owners of Uluru. We do not have an adequate translation for this word and call it 'Dreaming', but it is more than that and certainly does not refer to what we understand happens while we sleep. It does not only refer to events long ago but to the whole of life. It is an explanation of existence.

To the Anangu it is the law. It is the explanation of all things that happened in the past and are happening now.

To say my meeting with the Sahms was more than a mere coincidence is to say it was Tjukurpa encompassing even the movements of thoughts and desires of a transient *piranpa,* the Anangu word for 'white fella'.

Tjukurpa involves natural features like creeks, hills, claypens, rockholes, snakes and mountains and also people and their actions of hunting, marrying, dancing and working. So the very fact of our entering this land of the Pitjantjantjara includes us in the Tjukurpa even if only temporarily.

4

THE 'ALICE', A HELICOPTER SURPRISE AND THE ROAD NORTH

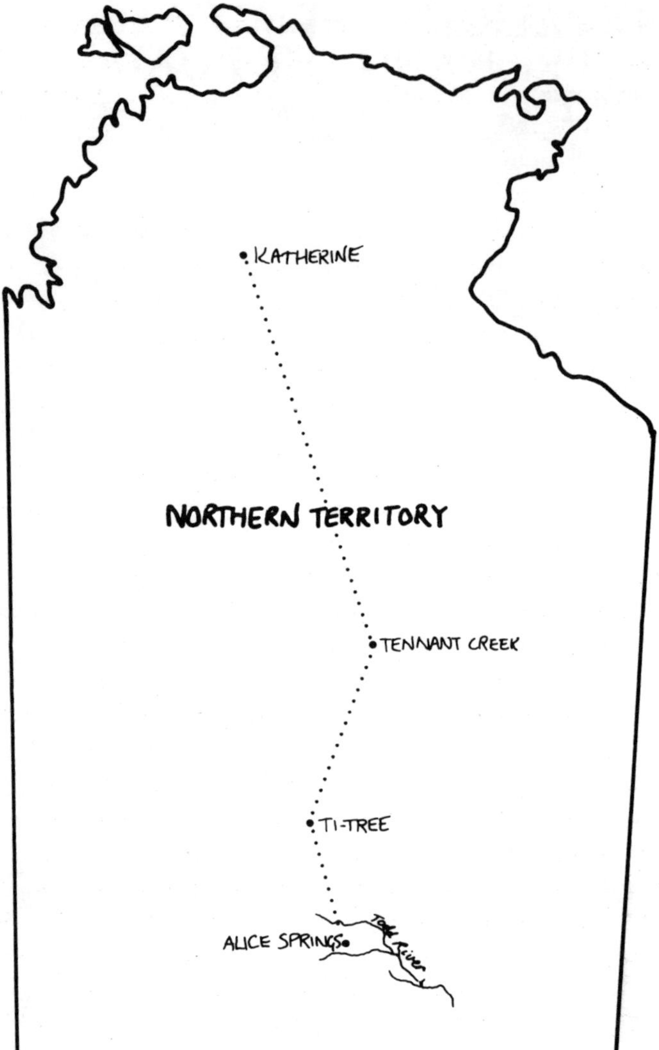
KATHERINE
NORTHERN TERRITORY
TENNANT CREEK
TI-TREE
ALICE SPRINGS
Todd River

Arrival in Alice Springs at 4.00 p.m. Saturday is not a propitious time. The town, named for Alice Todd, wife of Charles Todd of Overland Telegraph fame, is quite deserted and it is only with luck and a deal of muscle-power lugging bags that I manage to find accommodation. Alice Springs is the home of the Flying Doctor Service and the School of the Air, but these are not open for visits during the weekend. Like other parts of the Outback, Alice Springs has zapped into the present with its new-look mall and booming tourist industry. This is probably why it appears to be so dreary when I arrive. The shops are all closed. Staring back at me are the high blank walls of closed supermarkets, closed offices and closed laundromats. The town appears to have no character left now that it has had a face lift but maybe it will develop with time. A few dismayed tourists like me sit at little tables outside the ice-cream shop and look at each other, carefully avoiding looking at the occasional Aborigine who comes by; all of us have obviously been well trained in the avoidance game after a few days at Yulara.

The woman behind the desk at the Tourist Information Centre in the new, grand, two-decker shopping complex served by escalators is helpful but regrets the time of my visit.

'You should have come next weekend for the Todd River Races. We call it Henley-on-Todd. It's a race along the bed of the river in bottomless boats. Men stand inside and run like mad. They drink a lot of beer too! The whole place will be swarming with tourists.'

But being an Aussiepass person and stuck with the coachline's schedules I have to miss it. You can't see everything.

I have a look at the Todd River which flanks one side of the town and is also an ancient river like the Finke, and sand only. I do not see any of the Aborigines who reputedly use it as their outdoor beer garden. In the street some of them look at me sadly as I avoid their eyes. What do they think about it all? Do they wonder why we treat them as non-people?

What do overseas tourists think of Alice Springs, I wonder. It must be the same disappointment to them as it is to me. Can this really be the town in Neville Shute's novel, *A Town Like Alice*? An art show in an old stone building, formerly the Residency, gives some solace. Photographs of the area and its people are tastefully presented and on the floor is a railed-off sand painting by Clifford Possum, or Tjapaltjarri. It depicts the honey ant dreaming. A roundel in the centre is near Mt Allen and the parallel lines show the path of the honey ants in their journeys through the surrounding countryside. Women digging for honey ants are also indicated and the ants themselves are shown in their many stages of evolution. According to the handout these stories are thousands of years old and have been passed from generation to generation by means of such story lessons in the sand. Clifford learned the story from his grandfather, and is just leaving as I arrive. His quiet dignity and calm soothe me and I am able to see beyond the mall and shopping complexes of modern Alice Springs. I remember that the Flying Doctor still gets people to hospital faster sometimes than in cities like Sydney and that the School of the Air links children in classrooms separated by distances of up to 5000 kilometres.

Looking at structures like the new shiny bus terminal which replaces the old Turner House, and the Stuart Arms Bistro and Tavern which stands on the site of an old hotel that once had a great complement of bold bushies only too happy to tell tales of the past to eager tourists in search of the Outback, one wonders if the Alice Springs developers have not killed the very goose that gave them their golden eggs. Do visitors from New York and Tokyo really come all this way to be served Manhattans and sake?

Sunday afternoon at four I set off again, this time for Darwin, a journey of 1522 kilometres that will take approximately eighteen hours. I'm learning how to make my luggage more compact and what to stow beneath the bus and what to keep with me. My pillow is only needed at night so it can stay below until we get to Three Ways and then be swapped with the heavy camera bag. Breakfast at Katherine will reverse the stowage. Such petty matters assume great importance when living space is a reclining seat with a string bag holder on the rear of the seat in front and very little room on the floor — especially during the night when every centimetre of space is needed in order to curl up into a sleeping position.

Dave is our driver again and there are two or three of us who remember him from the drive to Yulara; we are welcomed like old friends. He will take us as far as Three Ways and then turn right for Mt Isa in Queensland. Not far out of Alice he draws our attention to a sign pointing to Pichie Richie Pass. Quite often wags from the town paint out the initial letters leaving you know what!

At about 6.00 p.m. the coach stops in the middle of nowhere, not even a tree in sight, and a young boy gets off with his schoolbag. 'Wherever is he going?' we all think. Then, before the coach can get under way again there is a flap-flap whirring sound and down comes a helicopter to collect him. He is going home from school in Alice Springs and passengers give him a cheer.

At 6.40 we pull in to Ti-Tree for a T and P stop and discover that it is the most central pub on the continent of Australia. We set off again and Dave is earbashed by a woman on her way back to a station up past Barra (Barrow Creek) where she is the cook. She often makes the four-hour trip to Alice Springs to go shopping. It's dark when she gets off, once again in the middle of nowhere, and we wait until a truck comes out of the gloom to pick her up.

Barrow Creek holds an infamous place in the history of the Northern Territory. In 1874 a group of Aborigines thought to be friendly but who harboured deep resentment against white intrusion on their land, attacked Barrow Creek telegraph station killing the station master and another man. A punitive expedition was sent out from Adelaide and the *Advertiser* wrote that 'Retribution, to be useful, must be sharp, swift and severe', and so it was. For two months troopers scoured the surrounding countryside shooting Aborigines indiscriminately, killing about fifty of them. White man's fury knew no bounds and there was little criticism of these massacres of men, women and children.

Now on to the Peko Wallsend town of Tennant Creek. It has a prosperous air. Nobel's Knob is the particular bounty here with its large deposits of copper, gold and silver. Tennant Creek has always had something to it, say the locals, making it different from other outback towns. Payable gold was first found in 1932 by Jack Noble and Ralf Hadlock. A year later Kaczinski and Bohning pegged the great Peko mine and the old telegraph station outpost was off and away. By 1935 Peko was producing two-thirds of the Territory's gold output. Prospects were great but the biggest problem was the lack of water. Says an early pioneer, Betty Richards, 'It was hard to feel well because of feeling grubby all the time. But it was a pleasant place to live because everyone was so friendly.' In his book, *Far Country,* Alan Powell comments, 'Tennant Creek people still testify to the thriving social life of their town and strangers still stare in silent wonder.'

No movies on this part of the trip but Dave puts on his favourite music for us, 'Rhapsody in Blue'. And now we pull in to the worst roadhouse I have ever seen, at Three Ways. Smelly toilets, cockroaches everywhere, waiters and waitresses intoxicated and awful food. Dave says it's always like that. They can't keep staff. It is run by Shell and has a monopoly on all the traffic coming from Darwin, Queensland and the south.

Passengers travelling on to Queensland change coaches here and there is nowhere to sit nor any place to store luggage during the one hour stopover. I say goodbye to those I know, amid grumbles, and return to my coach and the overnight journey to Katherine which we reach at 6.00 a.m.

Here I take breakfast with an exchange school teacher from San Antonio, Texas who is teaching at Elizabeth in South Australia. She and her son are making a ten-day trip to Kakadu and Darwin. She is enjoying the experience of teaching in Australia and comments that although Elizabeth is a pretty town it's a very tough locality underneath. The trip so far reminds her a lot of Texas.

5

DARWIN: AUSTRALIA'S FRONT DOOR, ESCAPE CLIFFS, CROCODILES AND SNAKES

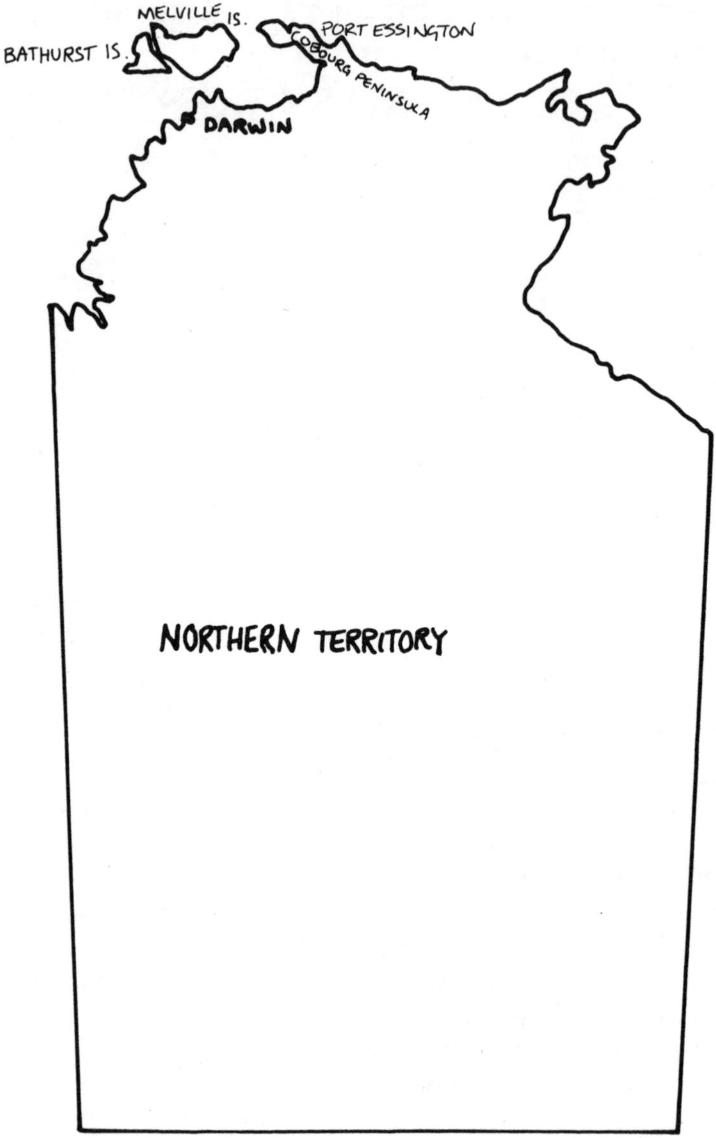
MELVILLE IS.
BATHURST IS.
PORT ESSINGTON
COBOURG PENINSULA
DARWIN
NORTHERN TERRITORY

Darwin just before lunch. This is a fresh, young and exciting city unrecognisable from the Darwin I last saw a week before Christmas 1974, when the devasting Cyclone Tracy spiralled in to change this northern city for ever.

Buildings are modern and forward-looking and quite as 'in place' here as they were 'out of place' in Alice Springs. It seems to have a great awareness of its own identity with its pretty state flag — black and desert red overlaid with the Southern Cross and a white desert rose — flying from buildings and on sale in shops as replicas or on postcards. The main shopping mall in Larrakeyah is well designed with small arcades leading off laterally from the central walkway planted with cool shady trees. People stroll around looking as though they are on holiday and everyone wears shorts. Aborigines abound here and are of a very different mien from those in the Centre. As well dressed as anyone else they smile openly and obviously feel very much part of the scene; they are not by any means to be avoided or looked past.

Exploring along the cliff tops I see the old Cable House Museum with papers, photographs, exhibits and artefacts from the earliest days of the settlement. A display tells the story of the first attempts to settle the north made in 1824 at Fort Dundas on Melville Island, and three years later at Port Wellington, on Raffles Bay on the Cobourg Peninsula. Hopes for a new Singapore did not eventuate as the settlers were attacked daily by local Aborigines — the fierce Tiwis — food and medicine ran short, malaria was rife and both sites were abandoned. Ten years later a second attempt at settlement was made at Port Essington. The choice appeared promising as it had been described by Phillip Parker King in 1818: 'Equal to any harbour I have seen. From its proximity to the Moluccas and New Guinea, and its being in the direct line of communication between Port Jackson and India . . . it must, at no very distant period, become a place of great trade.'

Women joined their husbands, children were born but the settlement was not a success; it was beset with hurricanes, earthquakes, frequent fever epidemics followed by many deaths and madness. Its one bright moment was the succour it gave to Ludwig Leichhardt and his party of six who struggled into this oasis of white society at the end of their fearful fourteen-month journey from the Darling Downs. When the settlement was abandoned in 1849 the local Tiwis wept and cut their heads with flints as a sign of mourning. To their grief was added the wrenching sadness of seeing the guns of the departing ship shelling the fort to smithereens. Buffalo, which had been imported from Java, ran wild and became the progenitors of the great herds which now roam the Territory.

Some ten years before the end of this third settlement, however, when the *Beagle*, of Darwinian fame, under the command of Lort Stokes was exploring south and west near the mouth of the Adelaide River, Stokes and a party went ashore to explore further. The party had a severe altercation with the local Marananggu tribe and beat a hasty retreat, some with spears sticking from their behinds. Dancing with pain and fright their weird gesticulations stopped the natives in their tracks; while they were held at bay by these now accentuated antics, the ship's boat was able to pull to the shore and rescue the party before the stupefied Marananggus realised they had been tricked. In the ship's log the area was noted as Escape Cliffs; those early mariners were never to know that this very beach would become the site of the fourth attempt at settlement in the north.

In 1864 Lieutenant-Colonel Boyle Travers Finniss stepped ashore at Escape Cliffs as first Government Resident of the Northern Territory and set about building a fort and several houses. His party included surveyors and workers, forty officers and men, and two women. Finniss, known behind his back as 'BTF' for 'Bloody Thundering Fool', was hopeless as an administrator and the little colony of eighty people lived in constant fear of native attack accentuated by some indiscriminate shooting of the Marananggus under orders from

Finniss. Land surveyed was lost during flood times and as one disillusioned settler, John McKinlay, who earlier searched for Burke and Wills, wrote:

> To describe it is beyond the powers of my pen. A greater sense of waste and desolation could not be imagined. As a seaport and a city this place is worthless. Not one settler in a hundred could build a homestead on the land being surveyed up the river without the utmost certainty of it being washed off in the floods.

In 1867 Escape Cliffs was abandoned and the local Marananggu once again had the land to themselves.

According to historian Douglas Lockwood, 'Darwin was conceived in the dark' when Lort Stokes sailed into the harbour before dawn and thinking of his young friend Charles on the *Beagle*'s previous voyage and wishing he were along, decided to give the bay his name and so Port Darwin was written onto the map. Local Aborigines have long been known as Larrakeyah but Lockwood says the name is trade-Malay for 'lead in', a reference to boats coming into the wind on anchoring, although other historians think otherwise.

Stokes named Darwin and George Woodroffe Goyder was its founder. In 1869 Goyder, known to his men as 'Little Energy', sailed from Adelaide with a party of hand-picked men to set up Australia's most northern city. His enthusiasm and good fellowship infected the whole company and in three weeks he could report back that already radishes, cabbages, eschallots and cress were thriving. Wells were sunk at Doctors Gully, named for his physician Dr Robert Peel, and within four years the settlement was established well enough for Goyder to report back to Adelaide, 'I am pleased with what I have seen here . . . sooner or later it must turn out well'.

The settlement, like the previous one at Escape Cliffs, was officially named Palmerston and it was not until 1911 that the city itself was actually promulgated as Darwin.

Staff at the Ansett Terminal are very helpful and give me information on budget accommodation. The Country

Women's Association has dormitory rooms for $8, and family units for $15. Lamaroo Lodge runs from $20 but I settle on Larrakeyah Lodge, directly opposite the terminal, for slightly more. I have learned that it is important to stay as close as possible to the terminal and so avoid carrying heavy luggage early in the morning when help isn't available. Larrakeyah Lodge was once staff accommodation for Qantas and sadly about to be demolished to make way for a grander hotel. These budget hotels are situated on the cliff side of Darwin, close to all amenities; it will be a pity if the whole area is given over to the rich. As it is, the youth hostel is away out of town, not the best for people with limited time to explore the region.

The most exciting hotel along this strip is called the Beaufort. Designed by Australian Kerry Hill, it is in keeping with the youthful flavour of reborn Darwin. The style adapts traditional Australian building materials such as corrugated iron, stone and steel and rearranges them in ways not thought possible by the pioneers. The colours, ochre, blue and white are true Top End. As well as Japanese, brasserie and French restaurants and a take-away shop, the hotel also houses Darwin's Performing Arts Centre seating over 1000 people. More conventional hotels along the cliff side look strangely stuffy and old-fashioned by comparison.

Ansett offer me a four-hour trip to the local sights and we set off in a small bus full of tourists from Europe, Japan and Australia. First stop is Indo-Pacific Marine, an aquarium, one of a unique company of only four in the world that are operated by their own reef-like ecosystem: the fish live in complete harmony as though under the sea and are not fed or scoured but given only a constant supply of oxygen. It is run by Helene and John. Next we drive out past Palmerston to the Crocodile Farm.

The crocodiles are 'freshies' *(Crocodylus johnstoni)* and 'salties' *(Crocodylus porosus)* and in the care of Janine who shows us her charges from their earliest days, just out of the egg, until they became crusty old chaps of forty to fifty years. 'Bert', in his own swimming enclosure, is the most elderly resident and 4.5 metres in length. Only *Crocodylus porosus* enjoys eating us.

The farm is set in pleasant parkland with shady trees and plenty of opportunities for viewing and photography. There is also an excellent video featuring Janine on the job and explaining the reptile's life cycle, habitats and style. It seems an unusual job for a girl but she says she loves it and knows many of her charges by name. She adds, however, that she is very wary of them and says one must always be alert when working in their domain.

There are four crocodile farms operating in the Northern Territory. One of them, Crocodile Farms NT, began with a matched pair eight years ago and now has a holding of more than 6000 reptiles. Skins sell for up to $300 and the meat itself for $20 a kilogram. In Japan saltwater crocodile skins sell at $19 per belly inch. The Chinese put great faith in crocodile penises and gall bladders and pay a high price for both.

Graeme Gow's Reptile World is the next stop, back down the track towards Darwin. Clive the snake man puts on the best snake show I've seen. He handles some of the most dangerous snakes with ease and confidence and explains that staying cool and unworried is the key to survival in his job. Any jerky or nervous movements have a bad effect on snakes and cause them to bite in self-defence. The most deadly snake he handles for us was only discovered in 1975. It is the inland taipan, known locally around Birdsville, its habitat, as the 'fierce snake'. No one knew of its existence until cattle farmers sought help against some snakes that were killing their dogs and stock. Investigations were made and this new species was discovered. Due to the extreme heat of the region the snake avoids the hot part of the day and seeks shelter in the numerous cracks in the ground and rocks that are found in the area. It has a small black head and changes colour four times in a year from mustard yellow, to brown, to almost black and then to pale fawn. The one shown to us is named 'goddess'. The inland taipan is the most venomous snake in the world and has enough venom to kill 120 men. Three people are known to have been bitten by it and one, a woman, died. The other two, including the owner of the snake park, are still suffering the after-effects; the latter's kidneys particularly were affected and he has been unable to regain the 13 kilograms he lost.

Aborigines call the snake 'Cheeky Little Bastard with Black Head' — 'cheeky' being the word they use for 'dangerous'. Clive has always collected snakes and has worked for Graham Gow for eighteen months. He just likes snakes.

6

COX PENINSULA, FARMING FIASCOS, RUM JUNGLE AND HUMPTY DOO

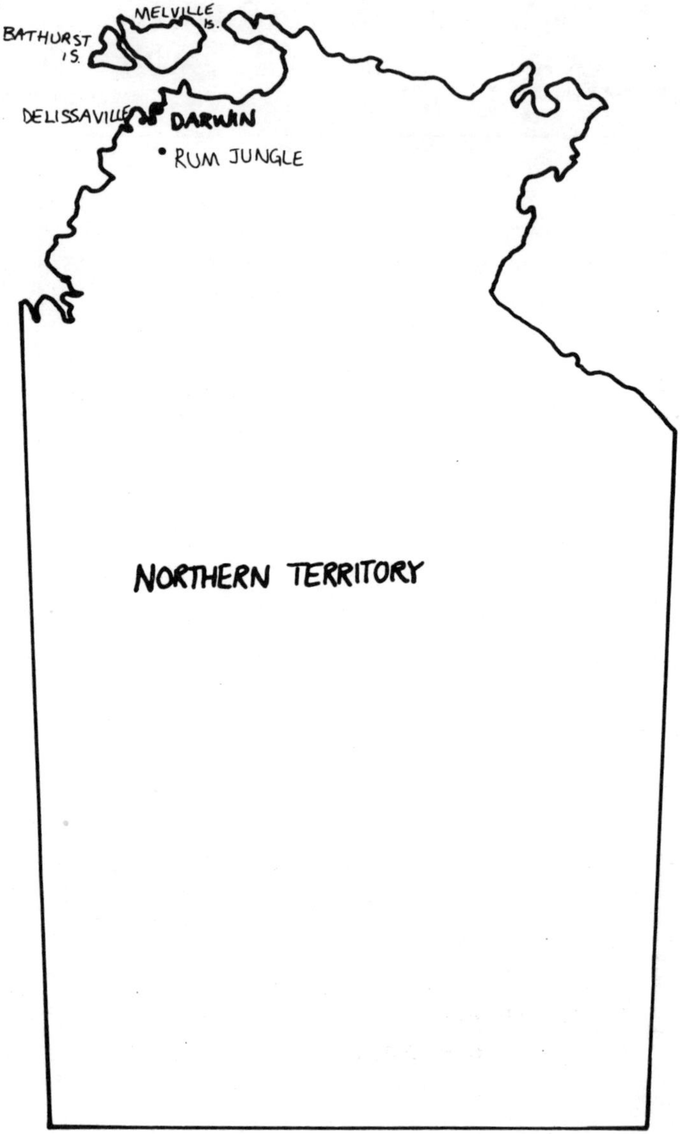
MELVILLE IS.
BATHURST IS.
DELISSAVILLE
DARWIN
RUM JUNGLE
NORTHERN TERRITORY

All night in the coach and all day with crocodiles, fish and snakes; it is time for a good rest and I take it on the full, going to bed and sleeping for twelve hours.

Next day I decide on a 'lay day' and use the chance to explore Darwin. Crisp, fresh and alive is the way it appears to me in the morning. Most of it is new, which helps the image. I decide that the trip to the Tiwi on Melville Island by plane is too expensive and choose instead to use the public ferry which runs across the bay to Mandorah on Cox Peninsula.

It is quite a long walk in the sun to Stokes Hill Wharf and in fact although I follow the directions on the tourist map it doesn't turn up where it should. A passing truck driver takes pity on me as I look out of place in that part of the dock area.

'You're way off lady. Stokes Hill Wharf is right back the other way. But hop in and I'll give you a lift. I've got some stuff to pick up there.'

The fault in my map is later explained by the fact that the port area of Darwin, Francis Bay, is under constant reclamation so what was water last year most probably will be land, streets and warehouses this year. My map is just a bit out of date, that is all. Always use up-to-date maps.

Stokes Hill Wharf at low tide is a massive structure of steel standing high out of the water about the height of a four-storey building. At high tide water laps the top level and falls eight metres at low tide. The ferry, MV *Duchess*, is tied up way down below and as there is a further half hour to wait I sit in the shade with a few other expectant travellers. Two are tourists from Perth, another is taking the afternoon off from work to go over to the Mandorah Hotel for a few beers and the other, a pretty girl from Alice Springs, is taking her daughter over to visit the child's father.

'We are not married,' she explains almost in the first breath. 'He wants to marry me but I won't live in Darwin. It's an awful place.'

I ask why and she says that it's no good for married people. All the marriages break up, so by not marrying she is avoiding the inevitable. The girl heading for the pub tells me that she was pregnant and 'due' on the night of Cyclone Tracy and had her baby in the debris.

We catch the 2.00 p.m. ferry which is also taking the school kids home as it's an early day. It's a half-hour trip and everyone is very chatty and friendly. The owner captain, John Mumme, is an escapee from the world of real estate and finance. He and his wife Jill bought the *Duchess* from a friend without much consideration and now reckon they live the best of lives on Cox Peninsula with the ferry run just enough to keep them in touch with the world.

We arrive at Mandorah which has a multi-frame steel jetty similar to the one at Darwin and now it's a climb up the three levels. Jill is there with the minibus to take the school kids and commuters home so I'm lucky to get a free sightseeing tour of the peninsula. Its most prominent landmarks are Point Charles Lighthouse and the ABC radio transmitters which beam to South-East Asia and beyond.

Mandorah was once known as Wangigi and the peninsula has an Aboriginal settlement at Delissaville or Belyuen, the people having been resettled here after the Second World War. The Delissaville story comes later. Bill Harney spent many years on Cox Peninsula with his Aboriginal wife and built a dwelling here in 1932 which the Aborigines call Daramankamani Billarnis. Bill Harney was said to be the only white man who could think like an Aborigine.

Miscegenation was known by the term 'comboism' in the old days and according to Matt Savage, a hard man and no lover of the law, black women are admirable over and above their sexual attractions; he further asserts that 'the lubra is one of the greatest of the pioneers of the Territories, for without her it would have been impossible for white men to have carried on, especially where conditions were practically impossible for white women, and even where white women have braved the climate and other discomforts the lubra has been indispensable to make life possible for her'. Savage, who married his Mudburra girl Ivy and remained with her and their three daughters, was ostracised for it; he adds that 'they seemed to have more brains than the men and were more reliable in the mustering camp'.

Although only half an hour and 8 kilometres from Darwin by sea, the land journey to Cox Peninsula is many hours over 250 kilometres of bad road. Delissaville has about 250 people and the thirty whites — adults and children — who live on the peninsula are made up of those at the Mandorah Inn, Radio Australia, Snow Casey's tin mine at Hang Gong, Australian Coal and Gold, Mike Foley's Transport and Tours and the ferry owner and his family. Those I talked to enjoy the isolation, including the kids, and wouldn't move for quids.

The peninsula got its name from an ex-Indian army officer, Matthew Dillon Cox, who inspected the area and decided it was ideal for breeding horses to sell to the Indian Remount Service. After a few months trial with a small number of horses he decided to overland a large number from Queensland and develop a full breeding program. When the first lot arrived at the Telegraph Line in 1872, however, the demand for horse flesh was so great that he opted for the quick profit and sold the lot. That was the end of the first attempt made by a white man to exploit the peninsula, but other enterprises were soon to follow.

Hot on Cox's heels came Lieutenant B. C. De Lissa of the 78th Highland Regiment. He took up 10 000 acres and began growing sugar cane in 1881. The South Australian government offered a reward of £5000 for 500 tons of sugar and feeling dead set to win this De Lissa installed a sugar mill able to treat 90 tons of cane a day, and built roads and a jetty 140 metres long to cope with the immense tides. The cane grew to great size but contained little or no juice. Within two years he was bankrupt and like Cox left only his name behind in the settlement of Delissaville.

Others, dreaming of the planter's life they'd seen in Malaysia, planted maize and tobacco but the only living things to profit from it were the caterpillars who soon gobbled up the lot. North of Darwin, at Shoal Bay, Otto Brandt took four King Hits in a row. His first cane crop was lost in a bush fire; the second was lost because his crushing plant broke down; the third was lost at sea; and when he finally got a good first-grade crop of tobacco there was no kiln to cure it.

The Northern Territory although geographically in South-East Asia is at the arid extremity of it. Unlike rich Java, Malaysia, Thailand and Indo-China, it has few natural resources and desperately poor soil. Nearly every brave attempt to farm the land has failed, Rum Jungle and Humpty Doo being the most spectacular of the failures. To some people they sound like cattle stations or animal parks but both were, in fact, agricultural endeavours which failed to succeed on a grand scale.

Rum Jungle, a small settlement south of Darwin was originally called 'the Jungle' until one night a group of wild Top Enders broke into the local liquor store. In the mêlée which followed a cask of rum was split open, the contents running out the door and down into a spring below. Much merriment followed as the locals splashed about in the rum-laden water, drinking as they frolicked. Someone told me this story in a roadhouse and it may or may not be true but it does have a positive ring to it.

Robert Poett planted 200 000 cinchona plants and 200 000 coffee plants at Rum Jungle and had expectations of employing at least 500 men within three years. In less than this time the plantation was declared a failure due to the seedlings being planted too close together. It never revived.

An experimental plot of cane planted on the Adelaide River was eaten by rats. A sisal plantation prospered but failed to get government support for a processing plant, so was abandoned. Experimental farms were set up at Batchelor, Daly River and Matraranka and failed totally. Maize, cane, rape, bananas, lucerne, Sudan grass and rice were planted but ill farmed and soon the areas returned to wilderness, the only product ever seen by investors being a pumpkin a metre tall and one and a half metres wide. Even the pumpkin came to a bad end as it was stolen on its way to Darwin on the railway, only to be found months later as a rotted out hulk! Vestey's Meatworks, a huge enterpise set up by the multi-millionaire family lasted only three years and ticks devastated cattle farming ventures.

The greatest agricultural failure was the Humpty Doo project, 56 kilometres from Darwin. Douglas Lockwood describes how a visionary American millionaire called Allen T. Chase had a plan to grow rice on a grand scale in this southern part of South-East Asia, traditional rice bowl of the world. His American view was that as a great part of the world's rice production was in the hands of the communists, the West should grow it in a democratic country close to Asia. Humpty Doo seemed the answer to his dreams with its location, its soil and its abundant water, from the Adelaide River and five other streams. The federal government gave its blessing insisting only that 25 per cent be held by Australians. Mainguard Limited, a merchant banking house, took up the Australian option.

Aborigines called the area Umdudu so Humpty Doo became the European equivalent. All this happened in the mid-1950s as yet another white man sought to exploit the Territory's riches. All preliminary trials went according to plan and the expectation was that by 1970 over 20 000 people would be living in the area.

The rice grew and the future seemed secure until bird word went out to the magpie geese that a great smorgasbord was being laid out for them, and that it was so lightly planted by aerial broadcast that they could take their fill at will. Chase's rice was not planted in the traditional Asian way by people standing ankle deep in flooded paddies but by the most modern techniques, using aeroplanes. The lightly anchored rice plants could not hold out against the day-long 'thousand bomber raids' of the geese. Chase was informed and he sent the now famous telegram to his Darwin manager, 'Shoot every Goddamn goose in the Northern Territory.'

And they tried to. Army bren guns were brought in and set up on lines to fire at regular intervals. Men with shotguns patrolled day and night. The geese soon learned which areas to avoid and returned to the feast. Humpty Doo resembled Passchendaele as the rice the geese failed to eat was blasted out of the ground by the bren guns. American backers like Art Linkletter and Robert Cummings lost their stakes and within three years Humpty Doo joined the list of agricultural fiascos in the Territory. Today cattle graze on the land.

Not daunted, entrepreneurs from Israel, Malaysia, Hong Kong, the Middle East and Sarawak all tried their hand in the Territory. The Tipperary Land Company from Texas proposed a huge scheme to grow sorghum, peanuts and rice. Unseasonal rains, failure in land preparation and planting techniques and lack of consultation over hard-won local knowledge soon brought this grand enterprise to its knees and the corporation went into the hands of the receivers. Uranium was mined for five years in the old Rum Jungle area and at the moment larger deposits are being mined from the Ranger deposits in the Kakadu area. These enterprises are different from agriculture, however, and have nothing long term to offer the Territory. Minerals are a non-renewable resource and do not regenerate. Rum Jungle uranium lasted five years and Ranger is expected to be worked out in under twenty. Much European exploitation can be seen more as rape and pillage rather than as constructive development for the future. The Aborigines have lived here successfully for forty to sixty thousand years without any government support. Now that we have taken over their land they have become a burden on Canberra. Things have got worse instead of better for them as well and on top of that their culture has been all but destroyed. And why do so many white ventures fail? Mining is a temporary success and tourism appears to be booming but can it last? It is true that most endeavours in the Territory since its annexation by South Australia at Escape Cliffs in 1864 have been fired by a determined optimism. In spite of the fiascos, natural disasters and war, the locals' optimism is one of the most admirable traits of the Top End.

Darwin's time of trial during the Second World War is not fully appreciated by most Australians because of the war-time censorship imposed in order to keep the nation's morale at a high level. Official reports of the time say that seventeen people were killed in a flash raid but this simple report is far from the true story. On 19 February 1942 Darwin was raided twice and 243 people were killed and 300 injured. Eight ships were sunk and the RAAF base was wiped out. Darwin suffered sixty-four raids in all, the last one being in November 1943.

During the war, army agriculture and horticulture flourished, with a string of farms operating from Darwin. These successful operations revived enthusiasm for the Northern Territory's potential as a food bowl but the success was not commercially based. The workforce was mainly Aboriginal, working at one man to the acre with little regard for costs as the operation was considered part of the war effort. For the first time Aboriginal men and women were paid a fair wage for their labour and it is possible that memories of these times are the basis of their present drive for better conditions and the assertion of their natural right to the land.

A stumbling block to the enlistment of Aborigines from the Northern Territory into the armed forces was their very real fear of reprisal. With memories of Barrow Creek and a similar massacre at Conniston it took some time to convince them that they could really kill Japanese who landed without being visited by a punitive expedition.

Just as many seeds, native to the outback, only germinate after passing through the heat of a bushfire, so Darwin itself seems to be a part of this native heritage. The Darwin of today was born of the ashes of its next trial by fire, Cyclone Tracy. As before, the destructive force came from the north and on Christmas morning, 1974, the town was hit by wind gusts reaching 217 kilometres per hour. Housing was decimated, the new northern suburbs most of all. Except for some steel and concrete constructions, the whole city was reduced to a rubbish dump of matchwood. Ninety-four per cent of the city's housing was destroyed and sixty-five people lost their lives. As after the Japanese bombing raid, the populace fled south once more and the frontier spirit was revived with garages along the way giving petrol and tyres on credit hoping to be paid when things got back to normal. Deputy Prime Minister Cairns flew north to inspect the disaster and promised that Darwin would rise again. The Top End had taken the attention of the South at last.

7

KAKADU, RANGER URANIUM AND WORLD HERITAGE

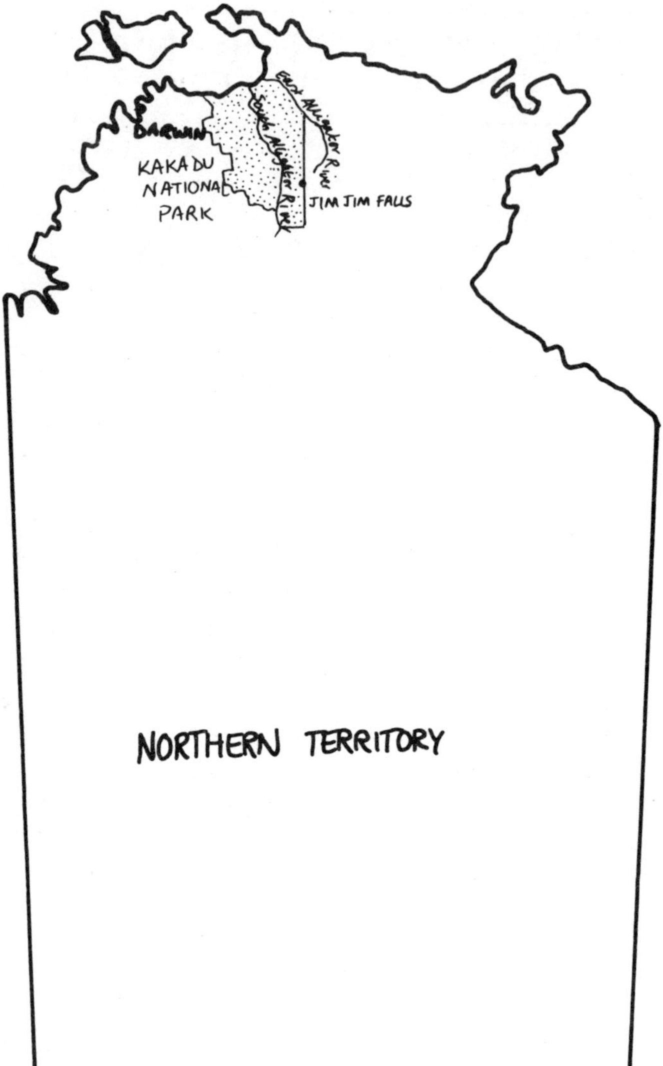
DARWIN
KAKADU
NATIONA
PARK
East Alligator River
South Alligator River
JIM JIM FALLS
NORTHERN TERRITORY

And now for Kakadu. I can only afford a one-day trip, a concession on my Aussiepass, and set off by coach at 6.00 a.m. on the road south then east past Humpty Doo and over the Adelaide River. The coach this time is Greyhound and we are admonished as follows by Frank, our captain (do you notice how well trained I have become, never saying bus or driver any more, always 'captain' and the first name?):

'There's only allowed smokin' in the rear of the coach and there'll be no takin' of 'appy pills, no funny cigarettes, no foolin' around with female passengers on the back seat.'

'Oh,' I think, 'this is something new.'

My seat companion is Frank Evans from Rockhampton. He is doing a four-day tour at a cost of $568. Touring Kakadu is not for your average Joe. But it is the land of the Alligator rivers, East and South, which are in fact infested with crocodiles not alligators, the name 'Alligator' coming from a nineteenth-century survey ship under the command of Captain Bremer who explored the area. The local people are called Gagadju (thus Kakadu) and Kunwinjku. Sadly my tour does not include Obiri Rock where the finest and oldest rock paintings are to be seen. I have read that they are thought to be over 20 000 years old and depict animals resembling the thylacine or Tasmanian tiger and a wide selection of fish and animals, continuing up to the present day with depictions of the arrival of white men carrying rifles. However, I do get to see some beautiful paintings at Noorlangie Rock but not before Captain Frank had given us another good talking to:

'You can get out 'ere if you want to and 'ave a look at these so-called paintin's on the rock. It's quite a walk and it's hot and personally I think you'll be wastin' your time. They're supposed to be very old but as far as I'm concerned I could 'ave done better than that when I was about three years old. You've got twenty minutes and don't be late back because it's a long walk back from 'ere if you get left behind.'

The paintings are in fact thought to be older than the Paleolithic Age cave drawings in Europe at Lascaux and

Altamira.

I hurry along the track only to become transfixed with wonder when the paintings come into view. The colours used are red, white and black and the drawings depict Namandjoig, a dangerous spirit. Beside him is Namarrgun, the Lightning Man, surrounded by a white band of lightning and with stone axes with which to make thunder, attached to his head, elbows and knees. His genitals are enormous. I remember what he reminds me of. It is the Balinese Creator of all things, Tintiya the Supreme Being. Tintiya is always depicted as a nude white male figure, flames emanating from his head, temples, shoulders, elbows, penis, knees and feet, a figure that appears in endless variety in magic amulets. Noorlangie Rock also has female figures with stylised heads in the form of quartered oranges. They stand together in groups, their hands crossed with one another as though about to break into a *pas de quatre.* All are depicted in X-ray style including the fish. Tom Keneally (in his book *Outback*), draws my attention to the fact that these women are used on the coat of arms of the Northern Territory and are described by the College of Arms, London, as having 'stylized internal anatomy between the indexed chief and base two symbolic representations of camp sites joined by journey or path markings in the manner of Central Australian Aboriginals . . . '

Keneally goes on to comment, 'It is as if the spirit woman, Wawalag, has been subsumed into a different sort of tribe and dreaming, the tribe of Heralds, the Dreaming of Arms.'

Uranium, the dreaded 'yellow cake', has been found at Jabiluka and Jabiru in the vicinity of these art galleries; another deposit at Narbalek has already been mined. Discussions are still going on with the traditional owners of the land as much of it is in an area declared national park. The Gagadju Association was founded to administer the royalty money paid by the mining companies and part of this money has been used in the building of Cooinda Resort which is our present destination.

First we are taken to Jabiru to pick up some parcels and mail. Jabiru is a mining town and very smart indeed with all the amenities a family would need when living in the wilderness. There are shops, a supermarket, hospital, tennis courts, pools, clubs, a pub and a school. Captain Frank explains its delights to us and goes on to say that when the lease of twenty years has expired all the land will be returned to the local Aboriginal owners and guess what they are going to do with it?

'They want the bulldozers to come in and flatten the place. They want it back the way it was before. When they could have all this!'

It is beyond Frank's understanding and merely reinforces his fixed attitude to the original inhabitants of Kakadu. I wonder, too, why the Gagadju feel so strongly about it all and if the story is true that the Aboriginal man who signed away his people's Dreaming to the mining company was sung to death by the elders of his tribe.

We arrive in Cooinda, at Yellow Waters, a billabong of the South Alligator River. A boat cruise of two hours through the wetlands is included in my tour and I notice that beer is limited in the restaurant area. Only so many glasses per person. The place is full of tourists and I can't find anyone to answer my questions. The tour runs strictly to time so I can't hang about to find out. I notice an advertisement for a bush tour with a genuine Kakadu Aborigine which costs $78. It's probably the real thing, so worth it.

The wetland area is about 2500 square kilometres and we join our flat-bottomed cruiser which will take us through part of it. In the wet season the Cooinda area is a huge lake: up to 2 metres of rain falls at this time, flowing down through the Jim Jim Falls, through Cooinda and on into South Alligator. Although it is all fresh water the area is inhabited by saltie (or salt water) crocodiles. The name is a bit of a misnomer as they live just as well in salt as in fresh water and are, in fact, estuarine crocodiles.

Our tour leader is Reg Joy and he has an encyclopaedic knowledge of the flora and fauna of the billabong. He first points out to us egrets and is well into a description of their habits and ways when we spot our first crocodile. Here it is on the starboard bow snapping at a half-dead fish. It flops around and doesn't seem all that interested. Maybe it's been fed too many times today.

Reg now takes us back to the egret story and we learn that the most prolific is the cattle egret which was imported into the country in 1933 to combat the cattle tick, and is now found all over Australia. A royal spoonbill now appears ahead and there he is, spooning away in the mud for tasty crustaceans and worms, quite oblivious to the clicking of cameras going on around him. Not far from him is a small coterie of wandering whistle ducks. They are the vanguard of many thousands of their fellows who will arrive during the coming months. Cooinda, being the largest permanent waterhole in Kakadu, is a haven for wild fowl during the dry season. Behind them, lining the banks like football supporters, are the black and white Murray magpies, mudlarks or pee-wees. We move down the billabong and the next extraordinary bird pointed out for us is the great billed heron coming out into the sunlight. It's a shy bird and not often seen. He peers at us myopically, wondering at our oddness no doubt. Near him is an Australian shag or cormorant. These odd birds don't have an oil gland so when they have finished fishing they have a problem with soggy wings, quite useless now for flying. We see several of them perched on branches, wings outstretched like Hills hoists hoping the breeze will dry them off so they can fly again. Without exception they have doleful expressions writ plain, 'Why me?'

More crocodiles come into view lying about on the banks in amongst the giant red lotus lilies. Aborigines find lilies an excellent source of nourishment as it is all edible — flowers, leaves, stem and root. It is the sacred temple flower in India and known scientifically as *Nelumbo nefuchsia.* Constant eating of this fruit was believed in ancient times to lead to a life of indolence and forgetfulness. Some of Odysseus's followers ate it in North Africa and forgot their friends, homes and native land.

The crocodiles seem to have no fear of the boat probably due to the fact that they were born after shooting was banned in 1972. They are now increasing in numbers due to the exclusion of buffalo from the park. Roaming freely the buffalo trampled their nests thus destroying a great number of eggs. Imported in the 1840s, the buffalo have done great damage to the delicate environment and ecosystems of the wetlands.

Roy tells us all about crocodiles and the three ways to save your skin if you are chased by one. First is to run like mad. Second is to climb a tree, but the fallacy in this method is that the crocodile only needs to eat once a week so he'll just sit under the tree and wait for you. The safest way to walk the billabong track is to take along a slow friend!

Pied geese come into view now, accompanied by *Pelicanus conspiculatus*, or the spectacle pelican, the largest pelican in the world. Roy points out a jabiru, Australia's only native stork, and the white sea eagle, our second largest bird of prey with a wing span of 2 metres. The stork catches barramundi and it suddenly strikes me that I've never tasted that famous Australian fish. The word *jabiru* is not Aboriginal as it sounds but a Tupi Indian name for the same Amazonian bird. Roy doesn't know how it found its way to Kakadu. Now we see brown diving ducks, and right in the middle of them a pair of brolgas. They are grey in colour and depicted on the Northern Territory logo, flying out of the sun. They belong to the crane family and are commonly known as the 'native companion'. This is a very beautiful name and I wonder who the poetic explorer was who so named it.

Black ibis, sacred ibis and glossy ibis graze together and are overlooked by the stately brolgas. Little birds quite near us, fossicking about in the weeds with bright red combs are the comb-crested jacanas, lily trodders, lotus birds or Jesus birds.

They have long, splayed toes that allow them to walk on top of the lotus leaves as though on water. A grey-whiskered tern flies in to take a look at us then darts away apparently satisified. Yellow masked plovers are not panicked by our presence so apparently there are no babies nearby. They have a nasty habit of dive-bombing humans who stray too close to their brood.

Roy quickly spots each new species as we come near. He points out swamp hens, pied cormorants and dark cormorants, better known as shags. He now describes the trees which border the billabong, the first being the silvery leafed paper bark. Its blooms are full of nectar and when it is in flower the honey-eaters gorge themselves to distraction. Well known as malaleucas, these trees grow here in as much profusion as do gum trees in the southern parts of Australia. An azure kingfisher begs our attention with an insistent tiny screech and all the cameras come up to record his beauty. Australia is headquarters for these noisy birds, of which the kookaburra is the best known. The azure is more purple than blue, as its name would suggest, and has flashes of orange. Now we see a blue crane and a white-faced heron and behind them a line-up of fat and wobbly Burdekin ducks. Glossy ibis stand beneath the fresh water mangroves observing us intently. Are we the daily entertainment for this profusion of wildlife who come to Kakadu on holiday to see the humans in their native habitat? Who is watching the watchers?

The fresh water mangrove is also known as the 'itchy tree' and its shade is a favourite resting place for crocodiles. The itchyness comes not from the tree itself but from the long hairs of a caterpillar which makes its home in the leaves. Hairs falling on human skin cause a fiery rash which has no known balm and can last for four or five days. The tree also contains a poison in the bark which can be extracted by pounding and then dropped into pools known to harbour fish. In half an hour the fish are stunned and float to the surface and are fit to eat as long as the gills are avoided.

This seemingly endless display of wildlife of infinite variety is one of the wonders of the world and has at last been listed firmly on the prestigious list of World Heritage properties. Its rich treasure of plants and animals has been protected for us to see now because of the love and care of the Aboriginal people and their Dreaming during the past 60 000 years. I feel greatly privileged to have spent this one special day in part of it.

8

KUNUNURRA, LAKE ARGYLE AND DIAMONDS

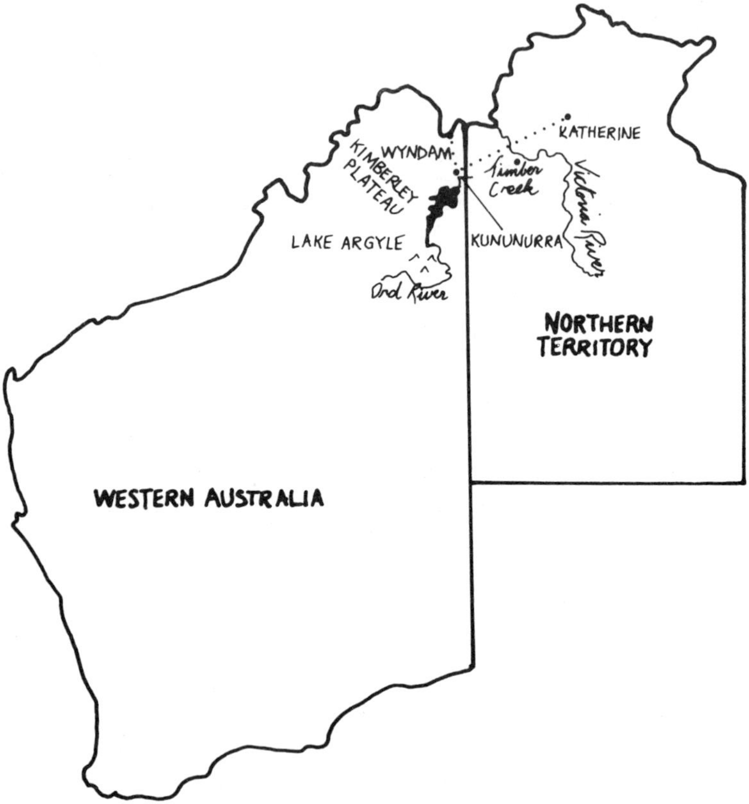
KATHERINE
WYNDAM
KIMBERLEY PLATEAU
Timber Creek
Victoria River
LAKE ARGYLE
KUNUNURRA
Ord River
NORTHERN TERRITORY
WESTERN AUSTRALIA

Friday, 2 November, and now to move westwards, this time on a Greyhound coach as Ansett does not cover this area. It will be a ten-hour journey to Kununurra via Katherine. As I am now familiar with this first part of the highway I settle back with my pocket radio and *The Bulletin* crossword. Crosswords are an excellent pastime when travelling as they keep the brain busy and also allow you to look at the scenery while you are thinking, unlike books which demand your full attention. The best radio signal is the ABC and this holds good all over the Outback and in the West. It's possible to hear such familiar programs as 'AM' and 'PM', the 'Science Show' and 'The Goons' no matter where you travel in this huge country. Unlike the ABC the commercial stations seem to be crammed with American-style evangelistic and Pentecostal programs. Why is this form of religion so popular in hot places? It's the same in Queensland and the southern United States as well as in central America and central Africa.

Lunch at Katherine and then the video *Survivors*, a soft porn movie about saving baby seals from the depredations of an international mining company. The dialogue is quite racy and our captain asks us eagerly afterwards what we thought of it. He could hear the words but not see the pictures and wondered if he'd gone too far in his selection. But the passengers all liked it. We are a captive audience and would like just about anything I believe.

The countryside is rocky and desolate and once again I marvel at the strength and fortitude of the early explorers who forged their way through this wilderness on horseback and with camels. We stop in the middle of nowhere, which is the only way to describe some locations, where a rough sign points down a dusty road to Top Springs. A dismal looking man with a broken nose gets off with his carry-all, looks around for a truck but seeing none, sets off walking. A nowhere man walking into a nowhere land.

After Victoria River for T and P we see another movie, *Rocky IV*. This is a bit too much for me so I put in my earplugs and read Conrad's *Heart of Darkness.*

Timber Creek comes up as a green oasis after the dry desert but I note the ominous sign in the caravan park of the danger of swimming with crocodiles. Warnings too that tents should be pitched a 'safe' distance from the river. It's a nightmarish speculation.

It's after school time and the roadhouse is full of little Aboriginal kids watching the in-house video. I feel far enough away from earlier strictures to ask if I can photograph them. The answer is not only in the affirmative but volunteers come from all over, happy to be in my picture.

We are just about to move on when there is a little flurry at the edge of the clearing and in walks a man pulling a trailer and surrounded by dancing children. It is Alec Wozjniak who, with his dog, has walked all the way here from Sydney. He has done it as a personal gesture and challenge and the point of it all, he says, is to link Australia's oldest city, Sydney, with Australia's newest, Kununurra. By foot. He covers about 30 kilometres a day, listens to the radio for comfort, pets his dog who seems to be bearing up well enough, and has already worn out two pairs of boots. Carrying enough water has been a problem but passing motorists often stop and fill up his waterbag. The most difficult part of the journey has been up through the Centre from Coober Pedy to Alice Springs. I wish him all the best for the last lap of his epic journey and sprint back to the coach which is full of bored passengers who can't imagine why anyone would want to travel like that.

The captain reprimands, 'You just made it. Nearly left you behind. We run to schedule you know. You can all put your watches back one and a half hours now. We're on WA time.'

So the ten-hour trip to Kununurra is almost a twelve-hour trip. I thought it seemed a long way. I wonder if Alex checks his watch also or if he just works on sun time.

We are now into the Kimberleys and surrounded by great, wall-like escarpments. Huge blocks of stone are stacked along the rims of high hills like ramparts against an invading army.

This landscape is not like the Outback, the Centre or the Top End. The Kimberleys to me are a lost world of great empires, embattled cities, ruined fortresses and devastated encampments. Is this where the world began, in this most ancient of continents? The rocky ramparts ranged neatly along the hilly ridges are too neat, too contrived, too specific to have arrived here *par hasard.* They are too reminiscent of ancient European archaeological sites not to need rearranging by experts. What ancient Babylons might appear from this timeless rubble? Aborigines have been on this land for 60 000 years; perhaps here are the last remnants of a yet to be discovered Austral Atlantis. Heady thoughts, brought on by the heat no doubt.

In *Kings in Grass Castles* Mary Durack quotes from the diary of her grandfather who overlanded cattle from Queensland through these passes a century ago:

> Of all the weird wild stages we have travelled none was more fearful and memorable than that through the canyon cliffs of Wickham Gorge where rocks rose sheer from the winding river, leaving a narrow pass for the complaining herds . . . broad volcanic valleys where the lava flows of ages past had left sandstone outcrops jutting like ancient ruins, or straight-topped sheer-sloping island masses of spinifex covered rock above shining seas of grass.

And today it's like that still in spite of the bitumen.

Arriving in Kununurra at twilight I feel I deserve a night in comfort so I book into the Kununurra Hotel when the coach stops. There are no taxis anyway and the youth hostel is a long way off. Outside, two men and a dog have unknowingly staged a diorama for me. Leaning against their old utility, dressed in khaki shorts and boots and wearing grease-stained battered Akubras, they talk monosyllabically to one another. The dog, framed between them listens intently like the hound on the His Master's Voice records. He understands it all. It's about his speed.

My room is good except for dangerous, slippery tiles in the bathroom. I take a peek into the bar but it is full of roaring boys so I give it a miss and take the *Kimberley Echo* to bed.

'Heat Ends Record Tourist Season' blares the headline. Tourists have apparently been stopped dead by the high temperatures. Also another group: 'Police say the Mung Beans are on the move as they head south for Broome to sit out the wet and get AIDS checks and dole cheques.' Itinerant workers are apparently not held in high repute. I read on:

> A school teacher at Fitzroy Crossing is charged with smoking pot and fined $75. A local JP said if he was on the bench the fines would be much heavier.
>
> A dog was taken by a crocodile in the Ord River at a favourite barramundi fishing place, hence the old saying, to see if it's safe to swim, throw a dog in first.
>
> While the national media conjectured for weeks about the 21st birthday present Mr Kerry Packer was giving to his daughter Gretel, the *Kimberley Echo*, being one of the most well renowned newspapers in the country, had the scoop. The gift was a trip to Kununurra. Gretel has always wanted to visit Kununurra and was very excited, after all not many girls get such a gift on their 21st birthday.
>
> The Desert Rat and Raelene thank all their customers for their service and co-operation whilst the proprietors of the Halls Creek Meat Supply. They would like the same excellent service to be extended to the new owners, Ken and Jackie, as Maggoty Meats will now be known as Rough as Guts Butchers Shop.

Next day an early morning start for a tour of Lake Argyle. Dave Nelson collects us in a mini-bus and on the drive to the lake gives us a rundown on the history of the damming of the Ord River. The name 'Kununurra' is Aboriginal for 'big water'. The huge irrigation project was built in stages with the Diversion Dam first opening in 1963 when farmers were encouraged to cultivate farms up to 300 hectares but to live in the town. In the early 1960s they grew cotton and rice but the cotton growing came to an end in 1974 due to high transportation costs, weevils and politicking from New South Wales and Queensland. Rice continued on a large scale but, as in the Northern Territory, the magpie geese soon learned of this new smorgasbord and arrived in great enough numbers to make further farming impossible. Sugar cane was also grown but ran into export problems in competition with other states. Today other crops are doing well such as macadamia nuts, watermelons, rockmelons, mangoes, cashews, sunflowers, peanuts and bananas, as well as common vegetables.

The main port is Wyndham which is 100 kilometres west of Kununurra and as well as being an export port is also where petrol and diesel are brought in from Singapore. This is cheaper than bringing them in from the south. Gold, silver, platinum, diamonds and zinc are mined in the area. The Argyle Diamond Mine, opened in 1978, now produces about 45 per cent of the world's diamonds and thirty million carats or 15 kilograms a day. Ninety-five per cent are industrial diamonds and the 5 per cent gem quality are pinks, cinnamons and burgundies. A one-carat pink, fully cut, retails for about $200 000. Just below Argyle mine is another diamond mine, not yet into full production but expected to produce 80 per cent gemstone quality. DeBeers have leases in the area but have not yet begun to mine. It is estimated that by the year 2000, 65 per cent of the world's diamonds will come from this region.

Kununurra is at the end of the longest milk-run in the world with the milk supply coming from the Atherton Tablelands in Queensland, a distance of 3100 kilometres.

We travel along the highway for some time before turning in towards Lake Argyle. In the distance the Carr Boyd Ranges loom against the horizon. Named for surveyor William Carr Boyd, who surveyed the area in the 1870s, they border Lake Argyle on its western flank.

Carr Boyd was no dry-as-dust citified surveyor but is chiefly remembered for his discovery of gold deposits at Halls Creek and also for his charm, wit and story-telling ability. Mary Durack writes: 'Father, always fascinated with a flamboyant character used up four pages describing Carr Boyd. Never, he wrote, have I heard such a string of tall stories . . . told in such a manner that only on reflection did one doubt their veracity.'

Even a story-teller of this calibre would have been hard-pressed to outdo the tale of the Ord River Dam which has now unfolded beneath the glowering ochre and black cliffs of the ranges which bear his name.

Wild camels are plentiful in the area and are currently being mustered for sale to Saudi Arabia. This may sound like coals to Newcastle but in fact the camels are worth $3000 a head as their generations spent in Australia have left them virtually disease-free. Feral donkeys brought in by gold-miners, on the other hand, are a danger to the environment as they carry tuberculosis and are known to infect cattle.

An extraordinary piece of information is that Kununurra, the last frontier city, scene of pioneer endeavour and gold rush mania has a current population of 4000, give or take a few Mung Beans, of whom 40 per cent are public servants. And I thought I'd left all that behind in the south!

To begin to comprehend Lake Argyle, second only in size to the Aswan Dam, it's important to recognise the immense volume of water carried by the Ord River, before even beginning to contemplate its use as a water storage phenomenon. Its volume of water, flowing into the Timor Sea, is greater than that of the Nile into the Mediterranean. The water now regulated by the Diversion Dam (1963) and the Ord River Dam (1972) irrigates 14 000 hectares of land but the ultimate area will be 76 000 hectares and the population is expected to reach 20 000. The river is 650 kilometres long and the great volume of the dam's water, almost 6 billion cubic metres, is eight times the volume of Sydney Harbour and is held back by a relatively small dam wall 335 metres long. The wall is not the usual concrete construction used in dam building but rock-fill piled up on both sides of a narrow saddle fissure through which the river flows. It took three 'dry' seasons to complete and the rock-fill was obtained by blowing up a large hill with a half million kilogram charge of dynamite and detonators surpassed in Australia only by nuclear blasts. It is known as the Kyogi blast.

The immensity of the lake becomes clear to me when we set out on Ron Cole's boat. Red, treeless promontories forming bays and inlets stretch away to infinity, the flat blue expanse of water broken only by islands and islets dotted here and there and over all canopies the blue sky, cloudless, burning and limitless. It is like exploring a lost world. Man's herculean efforts have put this water here but as yet the landscape has not accepted it. There are no green fringes, no verdant gentleness as one might expect with all this water. All is still, relentlessly ochre-black and forbidding. You can sense the rejection. Too much water too fast. 'We change in thousands or millions of years,' frown the rocks. 'We must have time to think. We, the most ancient of rocks were not forewarned of this brutality so go away and wait. Our decision will come later. We need time.'

But there is life on some of the islands and on the foreshores in the form of rock wallabies, euros and a variety of lizards and snakes. Ron calls the euros by name and feeds them with bread. White bread. It seems possible he is encouraging bad habits.

When the valley — old pastoral leases of the Durack family — was flooded, Operation Noah was set up by the Western Australian Wildlife Authority to rescue the many forms of wildlife now isolated on the islands which were forming as water levels rose. Volunteers set off in boats on this uncharted and constantly changing sea to rescue all the native fauna and move it to higher ground and at the same time to eliminate, by shooting, non-native animals such as cats, donkeys and cattle. The operation was a great success and no native fauna was ever found drowned.

As well as changing habitats the water levels also created new weather hazards. Winds funnelling through newly formed gorges erupted like mini cyclones onto the lake and boatmen had to learn, along with the wildlife, these new patterns of weather disturbance. Barramundi fingerlings were introduced but in the beginning were eaten by gigantic catfish weighing 36 kilograms. The problem was tackled by bringing in professional fishermen to catch the catfish and restore the balance in the newly formed ecosystem.

The historical homestead 'Argyle Downs' on the Behn River, built by Paddy Durack a hundred years earlier, was due to be inundated but was thought to be of too great a significance to disappear beneath the rising waters. Each stone of the farmhouse was numbered and labelled before the waters reached it and removed to high ground to be rebuilt as an historical tourist site not far from the Spillway. It was opened in 1980.

Many groups of people have looked to the Ord Valley as a solution to their problems, one of the most unusual being a group called the Freeland League for Jewish Territorial Colonization. The League's aim was to create a Jewish settlement 'in some unoccupied area for those seeking a new home and who cannot or will not go to Israel'. In 1938 the secretary/founder Dr Steinberg arrived in Australia to investigate settlement prospects in the Kimberley area. He waxed enthusiastic at the prospect of building irrigation works to conserve the torrential rains and applying modern techniques to turn this desert into a garden. His plan aroused great interest but the decision to implement it was postponed by the advent of the Second World War. After the war Dr Steinberg was informed that the plan could not proceed as government policy had now changed and community settlements of this nature were not to be implemented.

After lunch in the village accompanied by a video on the construction of the dam (compulsory viewing) we are whisked off in a dazed condition to see the reconstructed Durack homestead. Pretty on the outside but so small, with only four rooms, one taken up entirely with saddles. Doug Preece the caretaker agrees that it could be better but says that the people who control it are the ones who run the tourist facility down by the dam and they don't have money to make improvements. There is more to a pastoral homestead than four walls and a verandah but maybe that will come as tourism flourishes. Tourists deserve to see something more authentic especially as the stones have been so lovingly relocated.

In the evening I dine with chums from the cruise including VIP Jim Clough MP, 'Father' of the New South Wales Parliament, who keeps us all entertained over a meal of the freshest and sweetest fish on earth, the barramundi. My first! Two of us from New South Wales and the rest from Perth and Adelaide all agree to our total astonishment at the size, magnitude and beauty of Lake Argyle. Nothing any of us had read or seen prepared us for what we have witnessed today. It's an Australian achievement of the highest order.

9

THE BUNGLE BUNGLE AND THE 20TH PARALLEL SYNDROME

KUNUNURRA
LAKE ARGYLE
BUNGLE BUNGLE RANGES
SPRING CK
WESTERN AUSTRALIA

My Aussiepass is ticking away and I only have one day left for the Kimberleys. This day will remain in my mind's eye for many years to come for it is the day I am taken to the Bungle Bungle by Slingair in the capable hands of pilot Elspeth Gordon Brown, on a two-hour flight.

We fly 180 kilometres south over the whole length of Lake Argyle and now I am able to really appreciate its great size and beauty. It's like looking at a Sydney Harbour without trees two hundred years ago. Inlets, bays, harbours and cays go off on all sides and the islands that dot the main channel seem natural as though there since time began. Our course takes us over the vast pastoral holdings of Texas Downs, Spring Creek and Lissadell and suddenly, out of the flat plain, a distant huddle of red and yellow striped turrets and minarets comes into view, enlarging as we close in, to become the wonder that is the lost world of the Bungle Bungle. Ayers Rock, the Olgas, the Glasshouse Mountains, all are unique and here now is another treasure to delight the eye with its display of sheer rock walls spiralling upwards in lollipop colours to end in rounded domes of pink and yellow. There are thousands of them all set at different heights and crowding in on one another like so many living things. Separating them and far, far below are narrow gorges darkly sheltering palms and undergrowth and sparkling with the flash of silver water. On and on we fly, criss-crossing the escarpment from all angles so as to miss nothing of its wonder.

Elspeth answers my shouted query with a smile, 'No. I never get tired of coming here. I see something different every time.'

Eventually we leave this 'over the rainbow land' and head back along the Massif which presents a sheer cliff face to us. Cleft and fractured by deep ravines we can only guess how millions of years of weathering has worn away solid rock, leaving pinnacles 60 metres high. Following the escarpment wall we fall away to the west and soon come in sight of the Argyle Diamond Mines which are closed to the public and can only be seen from the air. There is strict secrecy at the mine and inquisitive journalists are sent off smartly. We circle round and round trying to divine their secrets but nothing is revealed. All we see are gigantic swirls of red grey dust and mountains of discarded rubble. Away to the right is a beehive arrangement of houses with a circular playing field, emerald green in the red landscape. The mines have their own airline contracts and fly in and out to civilisation without a look at nearby, civil-servant-bound Kununurra.

Elspeth says it's a Skywest contract with up to four flights in and out a day.

'They do two weeks on and two weeks off in Perth. It's a big set-up and we all think that things are really about to boom in mineral exploration.'

She continues, 'Tourism is the main source of income for people in this area. It's a great bonus and also good to see that Australians are interested in what is going on up here. It is mostly Australians; we don't get many foreign visitors. Only some Germans and Americans but no Japanese. Although there has been a Japanese film crew through here so maybe that will bring Japanese tourists when it's shown.

'Kununurra is a young town. The aviation industry is all young people as also with the diamond mine people and the fruit pickers in the agricultural area. The airport is very busy with up to thirty take-offs and landings in a day. We wouldn't change a thing. We like it the way it is.'

Last word on Kununurra can be left to Gregor McQuie, ranconteur, tourist promoter and entrepreneur extra-ordinaire. His enterprises, Triangle Tours and Cruises, and Kimberleyland Holiday Parks, are family concerns and his faith in the area knows no bounds. His house sits under Kelly's Knob, fifteen million years old; 'Conquer me if you can' says the sign.

A runaway from boarding school, Gregor got a job in Mobil Oil but that didn't suit so his father got him a job on a country property. Nothing satisfied him, however, so he joined the navy under-age and finished up in Tokyo at the end of the war. After various forays into the pastoral industry he invented a feed-lot with a man called Crichton Brown which was successful so he began buying and selling cattle. He bought 5000 bullocks in the Gulf country, moved them to Queensland, New South Wales and Victoria, but couldn't sell them. He became interested in cotton with some American friends and flew round Australia with them ending up in Wee Waa where they later grew the first cotton in Australia. But he had his eye on the Ord and the Kimberleys. He sold up everything and headed for the Ord with his wife and three kids. They took the train to Perth which was a bush town in those days and applied for land on the Ord but missed out on a grant. Undaunted they drove up to where the bitumen ended at Carnarvon and the road was no more than a bullock track. He'd promised the family motels but of course there weren't any; they camped out all the way.

'So we got here, to what is Kununurra today but there was nothing. Stinking hot, no water, no hotels. I got this house through my War Service loan. Then I went into everything that was going. Delivery, pick-up, farming, cattle, water business and tours. We were the first to take tours on the Lake in '62. The planes got bigger and bigger bringing in more and more people and then we got the buses and on that I founded my tour and cruise business. Everybody hated the visitor but I saw the visitor as the pipeline to everything we needed so I started to love the visitor and opened Kimberleyland Holiday Camp. It has boomed.

'People outside have also been led to believe that the irrigation farms here are white elephants. This is so far from the truth as to be laughable. I criticise the last few governments in Canberra for not realising what a vast treasure chest they own in the latitudes north of the 20th parallel. That is where the wealth of the nation now lies. Argyle Diamond Mines is one example. We've turned dry river beds that dreamed of water for most of the time into rivers that flow with water every second of every minute of every day of every year. Two-thirds of the nation's water resources lie north of latitude 20°. Our main resource is the monsoon, lying as we do about 13° south of the Equator. Our main rains are in January, February and March and our catchment areas are unique. The introduction of Landsat, high tech, plus photography has destroyed the old academic theories that we don't have land to irrigate in Australia. No suitable dam sites or water resources. A guy called Davidson wrote a book titled *The Northern Myth* and said these things could not happen here. But he has been proved wrong.

'When you look in retrospect at things that have been achieved here in the last quarter of a century you see things that have not been achieved anywhere else in the world. This place is working. The engineering structures for the conserving of water that will not silt up have been achieved and are working. The re-introduction of birds and native wild life and the flora of the area has worked. The great challenge of tropical agriculture has been taken on here and the things that have been produced and the yields are rewriting the books of agronomy. The breeder is starting to breed for an environment. He has learned something brand new in his technology. We now know what sort of fertilisers to use. How to use the water and how not to use it. We have learned how to flush out our tailings into the tidal waters of the rivers so they are taken out to sea and mixed up in the ocean, and come in with a fresh load on the next tide. We are not polluting the environment. We are not overloading our systems with saline.

'With the harnessing of our water resources in the Ord River we can now start to play a part in the future of the Pacific Rim countries, Russia, China, Japan, Taiwan, Malaya, Indo-China, Philippines, PNG, and the Pacific, North and South Korea and the Indonesian archipelago.'

I ask Gregor why he thinks that all these options are virtually unknown and go unreported in the eastern states: I have heard little or nothing about the Ord for years except for hearing that it was a failure. Gregor is interested in my query and says that the history of the North is not taught in schools or at best dismissed in a few sentences. I remember now reading in Douglas Lockwood's book the wry comment that in his *Short History of Australia*, Professor Manning Clark has devoted one sentence only to the history of the North. Gregor feels that it is this ignorance of what is going on in the North that is the greatest stumbling block to its development. It is true that most of the stories we hear are about failures and about the gigantic 'waste of taxpayers' money' in schemes like the Ord.

The facts, however, are quite different. Oil fields in the Joseph Bonaparte Gulf off the Kimberleys are continually being expanded and have so far cost in excess of $2500 million. The smoko bill alone for those two developments was $210 million — that is, for settlement and development. By contrast the cost of the Ord dams, reticulation systems, the town and the ongoing development cost the taxpayer $184 million. Taxpayers of Australia could not even have paid the smoko bill for private enterprise.

'In the Ord we now have lakes and permanent flowing streams where before there were only dry creek beds and desert. We now have wetlands, man-made, that are equalled by no others in Australian history. The "Operation Noah" exercise was excellent except that people directing it made the horrendous mistake of taking animals used to living in one environment and placed them, willy-nilly, in another. Sometimes on top of hot rocky hills when the animals' natural environment was dark shady bottoms. The animals should have been taken to a new environment that paralleled the one taken from them by the rising waters, even if it was far away.

'The future of this lake and river is the prototype for others in Australia in the next 150 years, in North Queensland, the Northern Territory and the rest of the Kimberleys. We are celebrating in 1988 what we have achieved in 200 years from a lousy stinking gaol in Botany Bay, riddled with disease and we've done a good job. Enthusiasm, funding and modern technology put to bear on the harvesting of our water resources in the next 100 years across the Top End, that's north of the latitude 20°, will be just as exciting as this present Bicentenary. What troubles me is that by the year 2000 we will have seventeen million people and 60 per cent will be over sixty years of age. Australians will never breed their way into this country.

'Japanese computer programmers are feeding into their computers now, information that tells us what we will be eating in 200 years time, a 100 years or fifty. Do you think in AD 2100 we will be chucking a slice from the carcase of a bullock onto the barbecue? Or will our steaks be soy bean or something similar? Whoever controls us in the future will be those who control the sun's energy for 365 days a year and the constant water supply for 365 days a year and use the soil to its best advantage for 365 days a year and there is only one area in the world that can do that. It is north of latitude 20° in Australia.'

Gregor's burning belief in and enthusiasm for Northern Australia is quite intoxicating and I leave him filled with a Messianic desire to tell the Good News to those dumb heads down south who are living in total ignorance of this great potential in our own North. Traveller that I am I have lived in complete ignorance of this wondrous part of Australia until my lucky Aussiepass came along but now all that is being righted. I'll wager a kimberlite to a catfish that a high percentage of my fellow Australians are equally ignorant.

Waiting for my evening coach which is to take me south to Broome, I find two booklets of poems by Roy Walker, formerly a stockman on the now drowned Argyle Station. They are $2 each — a bargain. From *Poems* comes a tender one, 'Graceful Native Girl':

I have seen her dance
and this man knows
head held high
up on toes
exactly the same way a Brolga goes.

The last verse of 'Spinning Yarns' in the second booklet, *Bush Ballads*, reads:

I've told you all I know
Now leave me quietly and go
Just hop on your bus
Without any fuss
It's getting sundown
And I like to be on me own
Goodbye people, it's been nice meetin' you,
So long.

It's sundown for me when my Greyhound coach pulls in to the hotel and once again I am off down the track.

10

BROOME: PEARLS, JAPANESE TOMBSTONES, A CHAMPAGNE BEACH AND AN ENGLISH LORD OF THE ANIMALS

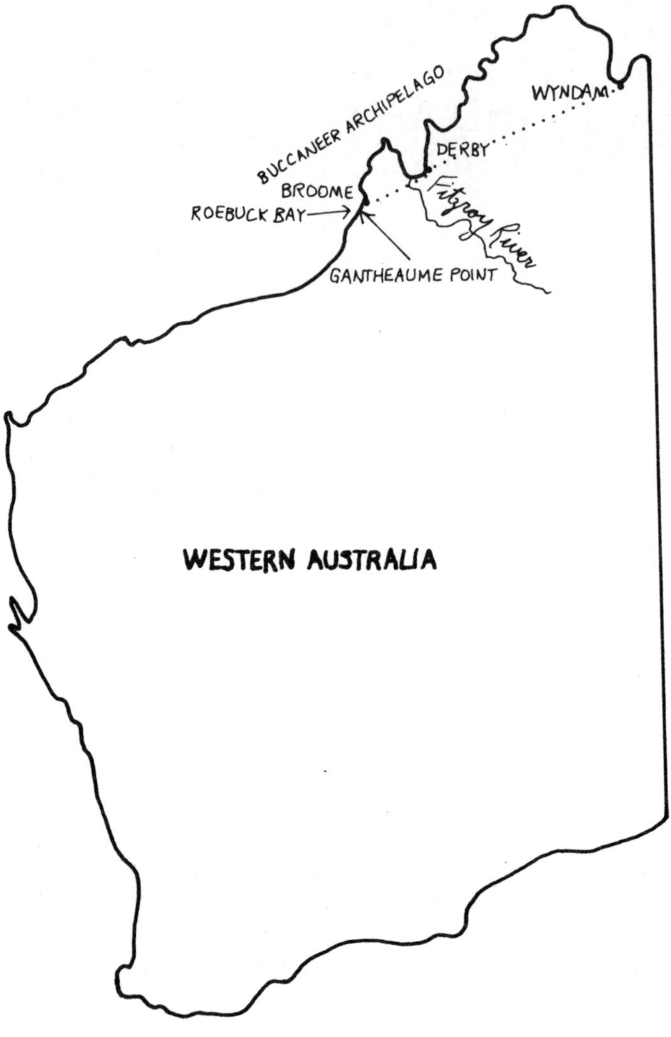
BUCCANEER ARCHIPELAGO
WYNDAM
DERBY
BROOME
ROEBUCK BAY
Fitzroy River
GANTHEAUME POINT
WESTERN AUSTRALIA

The twelve-hour journey to Broome is an overnight one and takes me through Wyndham, Halls Creek, Fitzroy Crossing and Derby. I am sorry not to stop off in any of these towns but nevertheless bone up on their histories. Wyndham, named for the son of Sir Frederick Napier Broome, was founded in 1886 when the Kimberley goldfields were proclaimed. It was the gateway to the Halls Creek gold diggings, and at that time sported eight hotels. A deepwater port, it lies at the mouth of the King River and is 104 kilometres from the open sea. In the days of the great pioneering families like the Duracks it was the export port for their beef and is still such a port today with processed meat going to England, America, and Asia.

During the Second World War Wyndham was twice bombed by the Japanese and more recently has been landfall for various boatloads of refugees from Vietnam. The masthead on its tourist brochures proclaims it 'The Top Town of Western Australia' and indeed it is, latitudinally. All I see is the roadhouse at the turn-off so this book information has to suffice until I can come back with more time.

Later we pause to let off some stockmen at Turkey Creek, a small settlement with the air of being a pretty wild and woolly place. Can't say why except it looks as though it is about to start up, even though it is ten o'clock at night.

Our movie is *Voyage to the Bottom of the Sea* and as we are travelling through country that has been described as the end of the earth it seems appropriate. The film has a soporific effect on me so that I sleep right through Halls Creek thus missing the place that had drawn 10 000 gold-fevered men to a life of dashed hopes and lost dreams, their lasting monument being a mountain of empty bottles. The place was named for Charles Hall a prospector who found a 28-ounce nugget on Christmas Day, 1886. His reward for finding gold was 500 pounds and on top of that he managed to sell the nugget for 100 pounds.

Fitzroy Crossing, the let-down point for Noonkanbah — scene of recent confrontation between Aborigines and mining companies — we pass in the deep of night and I finally come to life again as we cruise into Derby at 4.30 a.m.

Derby is a pretty little town of white buildings and streets lined with red flowering poinciana trees. It is also famous for its boab trees and has an annual festival to celebrate them. Boabs are only found in the Kimberleys and never further inland than 200 kilometres. They are the 'upside down' trees and produce nuts the size of emu eggs; these are carved as souvenirs by local Aborigines. The nuts are a valuable commodity as the following report from the *Kimberley Echo* shows:

> NUTS FLOGGED. Twenty-five boab nuts belonging to a Wyndham taxi driver were sold to unsuspecting persons by Rosendo Karadada who had offered to 'touch up' the fading art work designs. Karadada was fined $100 and ordered to pay restitution of $170 as only eight of the nuts were recovered.

Boabs live to an enormous age and one in Derby is thought to be two thousand years old. The tree is hollow and was once used to hold prisoners on remand but now serves as a more prosaic bus shelter.

Derby lies at the mouth of the Fitzroy River and was declared a town in 1885, one year before Wyndham. Three hundred years ago the English buccaneer William Dampier landed at the site of present day Derby after naming the skirting islands which protect it, the Buccaneer Archipelago. This landing made him the first Englishman to set foot on this continent, a hundred years before James Cook.

The coach schedule leaves no time for exploration but I am intrigued by a van and trailer parked near us with a sign on top reading 'Righteousness exalts a nation'. Travelling around Australia on firewood are a Canberra couple whose gas unit extracts power from the carbon dioxide and hydrogen produced by burning wood. The car is stoked every 200 kilometres and they carry enough wood with them to travel 1500 kilometres. Although it was not their original intention, the owners, feeling the world is in a time of economic crisis, decided to link their journey with the Bicentennial celebrations and have mounted a sign on their trailer reading, 'Around Australia on Firewood. Pray for Australia. We Celebrate 1988 on our Knees.'

Derby was, until 1987, the site of a Leprosarium. Leprosy, the disease known to Aborigines as 'the big sick', affected many thousands of people, but now it has almost been eliminated although it is thought there are still some sufferers hiding away in the bush.

I arrive at the Tropicana Hotel in Broome at 7.00 a.m. The hotel is recommended by the coach captain and his advice is good. Coach travellers without reservations get in at half price.

But Broome, Broome, I'm here at last. Seven years ago when I had to leave my little house on the island of Bali, due to 'circumstances beyond my control', I had dreamed of moving to Broome.

Friends said to me, 'Broome is your sort of place. You'd fit in well there. Go to Broome.'

But I had not heeded that advice. I'd gone instead to Queensland and that had not been the right decision. So was it Broome after all? I set out along the dusty red road to find out.

There is no public transport in Broome so you must walk everywhere and this can entail quite a lot of 'Shanks's pony' as the town is thin and long and stretches from the caravan park at one end to the airport at the other, a distance of many kilometres.

Early morning walking is essential as it gets much too hot later in the day. Everything you want to see is on this bay-fringing road. The beautiful beach I had expected to see is kilometres away on the other side of the peninsula. I called in first to the library housed in an old colonial building, to see what I could learn about the town. I found two treasures:

the 1983 edition of Hugh Edwards' *Port of Pearls* and an exquisite little book just published by Magabala Books called *Mayi*. *Mayi* is the local Aboriginal word for 'edible fruit' and each of the twenty-five written descriptions of *Mayi*, which can be found in the Broome area, is accompanied by either a coloured photo of it growing *in situ* or a botanical drawing. The Aboriginal people can still live off the land as their ancestors did before them. Sandpaper figs, wild prunes, bloodwood apples, bush onions, and bush bananas are some of the plants growing widely in the area and the book offers a caution: 'Sampling the traditional foods described in this book is not recommended unless it is done under experienced guidance. Some plants in this region are highly toxic and may cause serious illness or death.'

Mayi is the first publication of Magabala Books, the publishing arm of the Kimberley Law and Culture Centre in Broome. The research, collection of stories, photography and artwork are attributed to twenty-three-year-old Merrilee Lands. On the back cover is the following homily:

> Mind 'em this country
> With plenty bush
> Long time he bin mind me
> I bin always have plenty
> mayi and kuwi.

Part of its appeal is its simplicity of style, along with the unexpected locations of certain plants:

> If you want to find Minijuru (prune like), look outside the Bowling Club on Herbert Street.
>
> Darlab (like cashews). You can find this plant outside the Commonwealth Bank.
>
> Gabiny (Vitamin C drink) is abundant along Gupungi Road.

Everyone should carry this book on walks in the Broome area. Maybe eventually we'll have bush handbooks for the whole country.

Broome sits inside a headland jutting out into the Indian Ocean and forming Roebuck Bay, named by William Dampier in 1699 during his second voyage to the area. This time he was not a pirate but a respectable captain in the Royal Navy and in command of a twelve-gun ship, HMS *Roebuck*. He careened his ship in the bay but obviously saw little future for the local terrain describing it scathingly as 'the barrenest spot on the globe'. His name is perpetuated up and down the coast of Western Australia: in the town of Dampier, Dampier Hill, Dampier Archipelago, Dampier Creek, the native flower *Dampiera*, and the area of the Western Australian coast between Broome and Derby which is known as Dampierland. These namesakes would astonish Dampier as he felt that his voyages were a complete flop and says so in the two books he published on his travels. The journals were a great success with the public, however, and inspired the famous satirist of the age, Jonathon Swift, to write *Gullivers Travels* and locate Lilliput somewhere off the coast of Broome.

Broome was proclaimed a town in 1883 and named after the Governor of Western Australia, Sir Frederick Napier Broome. At first he was pleased with the honour but on reading a surveyor's report on the area, where it was described as a mosquito-ridden wasteland of red sandhills peopled by itinerant pearlers and their attendant shanty town dwellings he sought to have his name withdrawn. His application to the colonial secretary in London was refused. The name Broome was retained and later became world-renowned during its heyday as the Port of Pearls.

Its most famous pearl was the 'Southern Cross' found by a young apprentice pearler, Tom Clarke. He was opening oyster shells and one large specimen revealed to his startled gaze a clump of pearls instead of one. They lay in their cradle of mother-of-pearl in the shape of a cross. It was a miracle — a manifestation of the love of Jesus in this hot, steaming, fly-ridden corner of nowhere. His boss, however, a hard-bitten schooner captain, saw nothing in it but a misshapen mess, or baroque, and tossed it aside in a bucket. He thought so little of it that he sold it for 10 pounds. Its further history has become folklore in Broome and there are various stories as to its present whereabouts. Some say it was taken to London and sold for thousands of pounds, eventually finding its way into the Vatican.

Near the library is another beautiful old colonial building used now as a court house. Built as the Cable House and Administration Centre, giving Australia contact with the rest of the world, it came into operation in 1889 when the link from Banyuwangi, Java, with Darwin was abandoned due to unstable conditions on the bed of the Arafura Sea. The beach where it came ashore is called Cable Beach to this day and is one of Broome's big attractions.

There are no public buses to the beach so I hire a taxi and on the way across stop off at an MOP factory called Buccaneer Pearls. 'MOP' is the commonly used abbreviation for the mother-of-pearl that once supplied most of the world with its shirt buttons. The pearl oyster of Broome, *Pinctada maxima,* can grow to the size of a dinner plate and from its MOP produce pink, golden and lustrous white pearls as big as king-size marbles. This oyster has unusual sexual habits, beginning life as a male and then, when about two years old, becoming female. After undergoing a condition called 'white sick' when it sheds its ova into the mantle cavity and while still carrying its own embryos, it can, within the space of a month, become equipped as a male once more.

The pearl factory is unattended and even though I call and bang about no one appears. Maybe they've knocked off for tea or a siesta. There are great buckets of MOP lying about but not a person in sight so I remember something the coach driver told us about Broome.

'Don't try to get anything done in a hurry in Broome. There are two kinds of time. Australian time and Broome time. Aussie time flows along quite nicely but Broome time sometimes just comes to a dead stop.'

Further along the road is the Japanese cemetery where over nine hundred men lie buried, the majority having lost their lives in diving accidents and disasters related to the sea and cyclones. The tombstones are rough hewn from natural rock and stand row upon row each with inscriptions clearly etched in Japanese writing. Being what is known as a cemetery freak, I want to know the meaning of these writings but my taxi driver is no help. Then, as though sent from some Nippon heaven, who should come walking down the path towards me but two Japanese girls I had met in Kununurra: Junko from Okinawa and Keiko from Hokkaido. We greet each other warmly and they are only too happy to translate for me. Each grave bears the following information: name of man; place he was born; how old he was; when he died; names of his friends who made the stone for him.

They read a few for me and we are surprised to notice that all of them were born in a town called Wakayama. Later I locate it on a map and find it to be in the south-west corner of Honshu. People from this region, about 60 kilometres south-west of Osaka, are still mainly engaged in seafaring activities and worship the God of the Sea, Namakiri-Fudo.

Some tombstones are dedicated to groups of individuals and one with an obelisk says, 'April 26, 1906. In that year near La Grange Mission, forty-one luggers were sunk and forty men died. This memorial was built by the survivors.' Nineteen hundred and six was a year of very bad cyclones.

Most of the graves have bottles embedded upright in their foundations and the girls tell me that this is part of *Shinto* ritual. During the religious period of *Obom*, graves are cleaned and flowers and sake left as offerings. This is followed by *Shoro Nagashi* when small boats are made from bamboo and rice paper and with a candle on board are launched into the open sea on an outgoing tide to purify the spirits of the dead. I wonder if this is still followed in Broome.

A lasting memorial to the Japanese who worked in Broome for over half a century is the *Shinju Matsuri* or Pearl Festival held every August and fast becoming a big tourist attraction. The town swarms with jugglers, entertainers, satay booths, tents, fairy floss and all the fun of the fair. Japan sends a diplomatic representative and there are two beauty contests — one to find the Queen of Pearls and one to find the Queen Mother-of-Pearls. And Mrs MOP?

I leave the Japanese girls who are going on south and continue over the red dunes to Cable Beach. We will probably meet up again somewhere down the track.

Cable Beach is more than worth the taxi fare to get there. Seemingly endless, its great white curve sweeps away to the south fringed by apple-green rollers rising endlessly from a sea of deepest blue. The sand is extremely fine and very white, the gentle shelving of the beach making surfing a snip even for poor swimmers like me. I fall into the green champagne of the waves and they bring me right in to the shore. I'm a surfie at last!

Just over the road from the beach is a zoo built and run by the eccentric English nobleman, Lord Alistair McAlpine. Some years ago while on a visit to Australia he decided that something must be done to save endangered species of Australian wildlife. He built the zoo for this specific purpose but opens it to the public. His employees look after a continually expanding number of rare and exotic birds and animals.

He has also bought up all available old colonial-style houses in Broome, not necessarily to increase his real estate holdings but to ensure that they are not bulldozed to make way for modern tasteless constructions, and is also building a small hotel for visitors to the park.

'I see Australia as a kind of ark,' he says. 'Conditions are ideal for rearing many of the animals that are becoming extinct elsewhere as well as in Australia. People will come up to Broome to view the wealth of animal and bird life that remains on this earth.'

Refreshed from my marvellous swim I pay the small entrance fee to visit the zoo, or wildlife park as it is properly known. Much of it is still under construction and when it is completed the low spinifex scrubland will be transformed into a botanical wonderland. I walk down an avenue of palms flanked on both sides by extra-large cages holding exotic birds and see golden shouldered parrots, macaws, rainbow lorrikeets, cockatoos of all descriptions and tiny birds flashing colours of opal. The walk through the park, set in 26 hectares, is along high-railed boardwalks keeping the visitor a good 3 metres above the animals and so leaving them undisturbed and ideally placed for photographs. Two new arrivals are a pair of scimitar horned oryx, the second rarest antelope in the world. Part of the park is set aside as a wildlife breeding project, using incubated and humidified rooms where the temperature is constant. Each nest contains an infrared camera which monitors the breeding habits of the species under surveillance. Artificial lakes are still being gouged by bulldozers and their fringes planted with exotic and local trees and plants. It takes only a little imagination to see how beautiful it will be in a few years' time.

Lord McAlpine has come under some criticism for another pet project further north in the Kimberleys where he proposes a cattle breeding station with visitor accommodation near Walcott Inlet. The area has been recommended for national park status and Milord's application is running into some flak with the Environmental Protection Authority which claims that once the land has been developed it will become too expensive for the government to buy back when the lease expires. Milord says he chose the property because of its isolation and safety from the introduction of disease into experimental stock.

The day over, I return to Broome to check up on the cyclones which have caused so much death and suffering among the seafarers in this region. It seems that above and beyond all other disasters, cyclones rank as the greatest and most unpredictable threat. Hurricanes, cyclones and typhoons are all names for the same phenomenon. The scientific description reads, 'a warm-cored cyclonically rotating wind system of tropical origin in which wind speeds of 34 knots (63 km/hr) or more are sustained for hours or up to several weeks'.

The name comes from Homer's Cyclops, the one-eyed cannibal giants, makers of thunderbolts. In spite of modern technology there is always the risk of an unpredictable arrival of the devasting wind and nowhere more so than in Broome whose graveyard bears witness to its destructive power.

In my motel the following instructions are pinned to the back of the door:

> Your support is needed to minimise the risk of cyclone damage. Please tie down all materials which may be picked up by strong winds. Keep a torch and battery operated radio available, with a supply of fresh batteries.
>
> Check condition of doors and windows and shutters to ensure they are adequately fastened.
>
> Warnings for cyclones will be provided by being broadcast by the ABC radio station at a quarter past each hour when the Broome area is under threat.
>
> Coloured flags will be flown at the following locations:
> Short Street — in front of Streeters Supermarket
> Museum — in car park opposite Farmers Supermarket
> Post Office — in Hammersley Street
>
> The meanings of the flags are:
>
> *Blue:* Cyclone Condition Blue — a cyclone is expected to cause gale force winds in the area within 24 hours.
>
> *Yellow:* Cyclone Condition Yellow — a cyclone/storm strike appears inevitable within the next 12 hours.
>
> *Red:* Cyclone Condition Red — a cyclone/storm strike is imminent.

The Broome Meteorological Office is open to visitors but too far for walking being 2 kilometres out of town. It has equipment which can track cyclones 300 kilometres away but it is obvious that Broomagens need the added comfort of ABC Radio and balloons to supplement the high tech.

One of the most unpredictable onslaughts from above to hit Broome was not a cyclone but an arrow flight of Japanese Zeros which arrived over the town at 9.20 a.m. on the 2 March 1942. At the time there were sixteen flying boats anchored in the bay, mostly Dutch Dorniers which had fled with refugees from Java, so recently overrun by the Japanese. There was no defence of the town and the Dorniers, with their passengers, were blasted and burned out of existence in a matter of minutes. All the planes at the aerodrome were destroyed including two Flying Fortresses and two American Liberators, one with thirty troops on board. In fifteen minutes it was over and the Zeros were gone. Broome was a shambles.

As had happened in Darwin many of those who could, fled south and the American forces were withdrawn. Nothing could have prevented the Japanese from occupying Broome, nor in fact the whole of the Kimberley.

There are no accurate figures on how many people lost their lives as no one knows how many people were in the Dutch Dorniers but estimates are that it was somewhere around two hundred, many of them women and children. There is an obelisk commemorating their death in the Pioneers Cemetery overlooking Town Beach.

The Zeros returned on 20 March of the same year and bombed the town, killing one man. Sometime later all the pearling luggers which had not fled south were destroyed — blown up and burned where they lay. This destruction was not wreaked by the Japanese but by the Allies as part of their 'burnt earth' policy. Broome in fact was abandoned, with only a small token force being left behind and a handful of male Europeans who preferred to stay.

It wasn't until the mid-1950s that Broome's pearling industry got on its feet again and ironically it was the Japanese pearlers who helped to make it a success. Many of them had been interned during the war and in spite of protests to Canberra by the Returned Soldiers League, more were recruited from Wakayama and with shell prices rising the fortunes of Broome were restored.

A fascinating postscript to the Japanese raid story is the mystery of the parcel of diamonds, reputedly worth a quarter of a million pounds. It is the story of a certain Dutch pilot, Ivan Smirnoff, stationed in Bandung, Java who, seeing the writing on the wall as Japanese forces surrounded the city in March 1942, decided to fly to Australia in a DC3 before the city was overwhelmed. Just as he was about to take off with a group of refugees an official handed him a small box and asked him to take it along saying it would be collected at the other end. Smirnoff tossed it in with his gear and took off for Broome, a distance of about 1600 kilometres, quite unaware of what the box contained. In sight of the mainland of Australia and over the Lacepede Islands he saw to his horror a flash in the sky which he knew to be Japanese raiders, the very formation which was just returning from bombing Broome. In desperation he tried to take evasive action but the lumbering old DC3 was no match for the arrow-fast Zeros. Strafed and machine-gunned it crashed into the surf at Carnot Bay about 80 kilometres north of Broome and the Zeros broke off to return to their base in Timor.

Three adults and a baby were killed but the rest survived and were welcomed back to Sydney by friends and relatives. Detectives then appeared asking for the diamonds. Smirnoff knew nothing about them and explained that he was lucky to be alive, let alone be the carrier of diamonds.

Meanwhile, back at the beach, a lugger captain called Palmer had found the diamonds and stowed them for safe-keeping in a pair of salt and pepper shakers. Finders keepers, he decided and arriving back at his base at Penders Bay doled out some of the bright baubles to his mates. Some time later he walked to Broome to enlist in the army and tipped some of the stones onto the enlisting officer's desk. Uproar! Palmer got into the army and the salt cellars plus diamonds were taken to Perth. Investigations later showed that they were only half of the original consignment and Palmer and his friends were grilled by the secret service but stuck to their guns that it was all they had. The other half of the swag was never found, but until the time of his death Palmer was known on the coast as Diamond Jim. The search for the missing treasure still goes on as tales are told of diamonds being offered to pay for food store accounts and used like chips in card games. This magical area keeps its secrets well.

In Hugh Edwards' book I came across this astonishing paragraph, proving to me how little we know about the conditions of Aborigines in Western Australia:

> The clinking sound of Aboriginal chain-gangs working on the roads had also ceased. Jack Norton, the superintendent of Broome Gaol, discontinued their use seven years after the war on his own responsibility. He considered them an outrage against human dignity and was rewarded in his faith when the road gangs continued working cheerfully and no one ran away.

And this was in the 1950s!

Next day I decide to venture further and walk to Chinatown which is the Port of Broome. Nothing to be seen of Roebuck Bay except dry land forrested with mangroves and long high jetties running out through the undergrowth. Luggers, frozen in time, strain at their hawsers as though anxious to be away but alas they are stuck hard and fast on the dry rocky bottom of the harbour. Broome has a tide nearly 10 metres high so when it is out the luggers are left high and dry until the sea returns. During my three days in Broome the tide is always out during the middle of the day so I only see stranded ships.

Broome is much closer to Singapore than to Sydney and has a distinct Asian air to it with names on its shops like Fong, Yuen, Wing and Tong and a telephone box with a pagoda-like roof. Locals look like film extras waiting to be called for a 'shoot' as they loll about on the steps of the old jarrah wood buildings, many with slight oriental casts to their features which betray their mixed ancestry. Outside Streeter and Male's building is an Aboriginal family so tall and handsome that I'm sure they really are film stars. All are well dressed and a beautiful dark-skinned girl has an astonishing thick plait of blonde hair dangling down her back.

One of the narrow alleyways from Broome's roaring days remains as John Chi's Lane and today offers art and craft shops, jewellery shops and trendy coffee shops, a very different type of commerce from that of the wild pearling days. In their heyday both John Chi and Sheba Lanes hummed with the activity of gambling dens, long-soup eating houses, barbers, billiard rooms and the inevitable girls for sale.

Before the First World War Chinatown had six hotels, three picture shows, six European stores and all kinds of small industries catering to the burgeoning population of over 5000 in the lay-up season. With the outbreak of war in 1914, the pearl shell industry collapsed as almost overnight shell became unsaleable. Banks foreclosed, lugger captains were ruined and the industry never recovered its former glory.

In the main street is a Ken Done shop and another which sells the bright beachwear of the 'Mosmanized' swank beach shops of Sydney. Across the park is a stranded DC3 Garuda Airlines plane which crash-landed in 1974 and until recently was used as the local government tourist bureau. It is now preserved as a tourist attraction. Sun Theatre is an open-air movie house which first opened in 1916 and is currently showing *Footrot Flats*. I might go if I can figure out how to get back to my hotel when it's over.

By a great stroke of luck I am going to see one of Broome's unique attractions, 'The Golden Staircase to the Moon'. This phenomenon occurs only a few times a year when low-water spring tides coincide with moonrise over the corrugated mudflats of Roebuck Bay. The reflected moonlight ripples from the rising moon directly to the shore they say, and who dares walk it, wins. Wins oblivion of course as the fast-rising tide would engulf the intrepid walker in minutes. I've seen the tide rushing in so I'll not be seeking this particular lunar trail.

Another of Broome's curiosities are the Dinosaur Tracks embedded in sandstone about 27 metres from the base of the cliff at Gantheaume Point. The tracks were made by a carnivorous species about 10 metres high which lived 130 million years ago and whose scientific name is *Megalosauropus bromensis*. Like the Staircase, they can only be seen at very low tide.

On a rock shelf above the famous footprints is a pond rounded out with concrete and known locally as Anastasia's Pool. It was built by Patrick Percy, successful entrepreneur and council president, famous also for his walking stick which turned into a sword at a flick of a discreetly placed switch. On retirement he took over the Gantheaume Lighthouse which had gone automatic and transformed it into a house for himself and his wife Anastasia. When she developed a crippling disease which prevented her getting down to the sea he gouged out a pool which filled with water at high tide. It is a gentle reminder of the past in this town with its turbulent history. Gossip has it that Percy's real name was Kelly and that he was a runaway Irish rebel.

The sandhills of the Kennedy Hill Reserve were a camping area for thousands of years for three tribal groups now called collectively the Mallinbar community. In a historic ceremony on September 1987 the land was officially handed over to the community by the minister for aboriginal affairs. For several years tourist developers had tried to have the community moved to other sites and would have done so if it had not been for the determined efforts on the part of two old ladies. The story goes that the ladies said they would chain themselves to a tree if the bulldozers came. 'They will have to bring cranes to pull us out!' they declared.

Their determined actions fired the whole Mallinbar community into action and now that they have legal tenure to the land they hold to be their own, their next step is to improve their standard of housing. They already have a meeting hall and a community office.

Horrie Miller is one of Broome's best remembered heroes. He built Australia's first private aeroplane to fly successfully and later flew in the Australian Flying Squadron in the First World War. After the war he ran a flying circus of joy rides and aerial displays but eventually, needing more finance, joined up with Sir MacPherson Robertson of MacRobertson's Chocolates fame who sponsored the air race from London to Melbourne in 1934. Together they formed MacRobertson Miller Airlines. His widow is Dame Mary Durack Miller, Western Australia's most respected historical writer. The old Wackett aeroplane which he flew is now preserved in the main street of Broome as a memorial to the pioneer aviator.

A new industry is about to start in Broome with the discovery of huge beds of king prawns. Known as the 'Grim Reaper', the prawn trawling industry is greatly feared in Broome and is seen as a threat to the delicate balance needed for the growth of pearl shell. The locals see it as 'slash and burn' fishing, virtually destroying everything that lies in its path.

In spite of the new-look tourism and prawning most people still feel that the name of Broome will forever be associated with pearls. At the entrance to Chinatown is an unusual memorial in the shape of a pearling lugger, the *Sam Male*, and three life-size figures beside it staring into the far distance. They are the men who brought the cultured pearl industry to Western Australia, H. Iwaki, T. Kuribayashi and K. Durea. It is in cultured pearls that this great treasure of the sea lies today.

In the evening I walk with others to a viewing point among the mangroves and see the moon rise from the sea at low water, gasping with my companions at the long rippling path of golden light that snakes tantalisingly towards us across the shining sand. There is for a few moments a mystical and almost holy hush about us and we refrain from making silly jokes. Then the staircase is severed and it's too late to get to the moon this time.

11

THE GREAT SANDY DESERT, PORT HEDLAND, THE PILBARA, OMAR'S, KARRATHA AND THE BURRUP

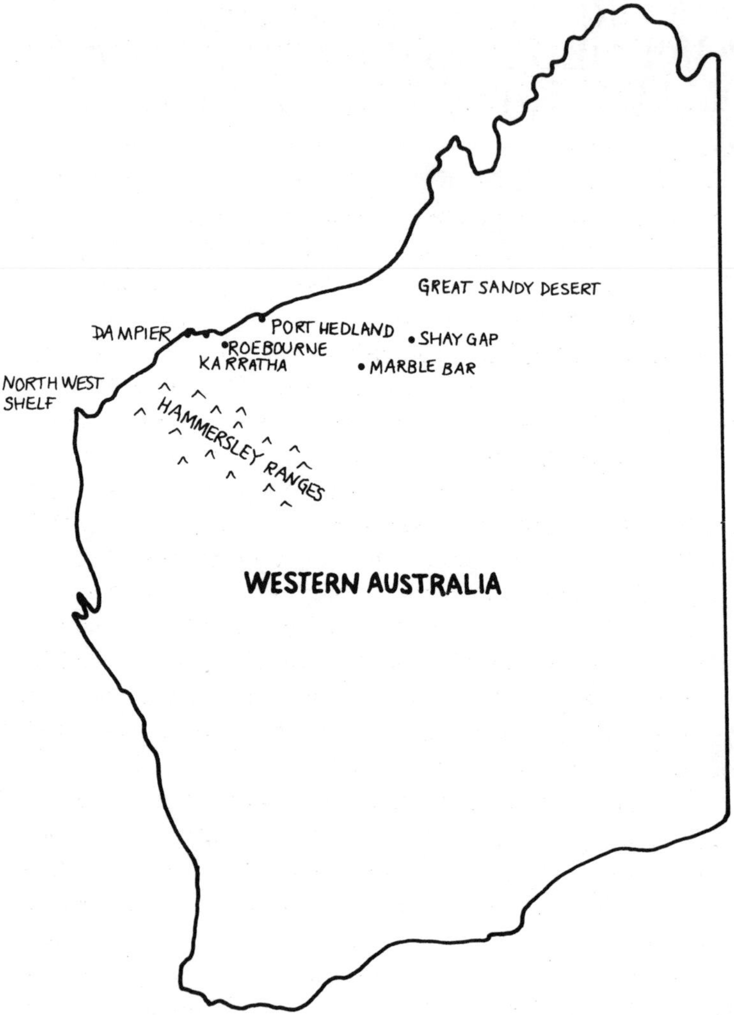
GREAT SANDY DESERT
DAMPIER
PORT HEDLAND
ROEBOURNE
SHAY GAP
KARRATHA
MARBLE BAR
NORTH WEST SHELF
HAMMERSLEY RANGES
WESTERN AUSTRALIA

Reluctantly I leave Broome at 8.15 a.m. to head south. Waiting at the coach terminal I try to find out about Roebourne but fail to get information on accommodation and the availability of local transportation further south. The best idea, I am told, is to enquire at Port Hedland which is closer to the destination. This will be a journey of about eight hours rimming the Indian Ocean along a road that skirts Eighty Mile Beach and is the seaward side of the Great Sandy Desert.

It proves to be the greatest stretch of nothingness I've traversed so far. Not one tree nor even shrub, just unending red soil desert with sparse ground cover of spinifex and pale green, weedy plants.

I drowse through a great part of the morning probably because my eyes are not accustomed to looking at nothing for hours on end and so the receiving centre of the brain closes down due to lack of in-put.

Eventually, round about lunch time something looms up on the flat horizon and proves to be a roadhouse named Sandfire, a word first coined by Ludwig Leichhardt in his journal. The name suits well as Sandfire is halfway between Broome and Port Hedland in a wilderness of sand flats and fiery heat. To one side is a heap of wrecked cars. Killed by the heat I suppose. Half an hour on we cross the rabbit-proof fence running east 200 kilometres to the Isabella Ranges — one of several in Western Australia.

Next stop is a roadhouse called Pardoo with green lawns, the beginnings of a swimming pool and reasonable motel accommodation. The lawns prove that all the desert needs is water. They serve good fish here caught nearby at the beach: Australian salmon from the aptly named Poissonier Point. I am surprised to find the two Japanese girls, Keiko and Junko, who have come through on another bus and are planning to stay in Port Hedland.

Further on towards Port Hedland we turn off to the mining settlement of Goldsworthy to pick up passengers. This road continues on inland to Marble Bar, named for its bar of pure jasper, and Shay Gap. Nothing to the west of here save mining outposts and desert for 1700 kilometres to Alice Springs.

On the outskirts of Port Hedland the terrain changes to one of oddly shaped rocks like great pimples and rounded breasts. Perhaps these are outcrops of the great Hammersley Ranges. Huge salt evaporators now come between us and the coast, their white pyramid mountains gleaming in the sun. We enter Port Hedland and I am reminded of Port Kembla, the steel town south of Sydney, except that Port Hedland is red with desert dust instead of black with coal dust. It doesn't look very inviting from the bus depot and I see that the Japanese girls have already changed their minds and are now travelling directly to Perth.

Port Hedland probably gets its name from a Danish whaling ship working in these waters in about 1820. The original spelling was 'Hudland' and was so noted by Lieutenant Phillip Parker King while carrying out a survey on the coast in 1822. By coincidence, in 1863 a Captain Peter Hedland surveyed the coast in the vessel *Mystery,* searching for suitable landing places for stock. He reported nothing suitable but nevertheless a settlement was made at Finucane Island and named Port Hedland after the captain. It seems to have been an unfortunate choice as the area was low lying and marshy and continually threatened by rising tides. Sea walls had to be built to keep the ocean at bay, and an 8-kilometre causeway laid to give access over the marsh.

Marble Bar's gold strike in 1891 lifted its fortunes slightly but it was the discovery of iron ore at Mt Goldsworthy, Mt Newman and Shay Gap in 1960 by Lang Hancock that really put Port Hedland on the map and led to its being called the 'Ruhr of South-East Asia'. In spite of its lack of beauty Port Hedland is a thriving city receiving daily trains one and a half kilometres long loaded with ore for shipment overseas. A dormitory town has been built at South Hedland where people live in modern houses with all the amenities necessary for living in the hot climate.

When the causeway was built in 1899 it caused a huge uproar with accusations of graft and corruption. The *Western Mail* editorialised: 'The road to Port Hedland finished with a causeway over the marshes some 5 miles long. This has just been finished by the Government and must have cost thousands of pounds. It seems to us a reckless waste of money . . . '

In those days the population was a mere 250 Europeans but now it is well over 15 000 and rising, all a direct result of the phenomenal iron ore finds of the Pilbara.

Making enquires about my forward journey in the tourist centre I am intrigued with the names of towns in the Pilbara, and their derivation:

Pilbara — a fresh water fish found in the area.

Paraburdoo — from *piru* meaning 'meat' and *pardo* meaning 'feathers' and referring to the profusion of white cockatoos found there.

Pannawonica — meaning 'the hill that came from the sea'.

Shay Gap — named for Shea, a pearler who recruited Aborigines in the area to work as divers.

Tom Price — named for American Tom Price, of the Kaiser Steel Corporation, who recommended the ore development.

Wittenoom — named for Frank Wittenoom, partner of George Hancock at Mulga Downs Station.

Karratha — Aboriginal for 'good country'.

Poongkaliyarra — Aboriginal for 'sisters-in-law'.

Newman — named for Aubrey Woodward Newman, an early explorer who died of typhoid there in 1896.

Goldsworthy — named for T. Tuckfield Goldsworthy, Colonial Secretary under Governor Broome in the 1880s.

Marble Bar — named for the huge bar of jasper found there in 1908.

Burrup — named after Henry Wood Burrup, one of two men mysteriously murdered at the Union Bank, Roebourne in 1885.

Wickham — named for the Captain of HMS *Beagle*, on its second voyage.

Roebourne — named after S. J. Roe, first surveyor general for Western Australia.

I decide to make my mind up about a destination as I go along and sitting back in the coach find myself alongside an English girl spending a six-month working holiday in Australia.

'I come from a village near Nottingham. I enjoyed staying in Hedland. You missed something. The youth hostel is high up on a hill and you can watch the huge ore ships being loaded with raw material. It's also a fabulous sunset. I see a bit more of Australia every time I come out here. This is my first time in the West.'

By the time we get to Wickham it is dark and it doesn't look very inviting so I decide to go on to Roebourne. It's an amazing little place which has been destroyed fifteen times by cyclones yet has a local population famous for its lively pubs and sports activities. When I arrive they tell me I should have been here yesterday when several people were taken off to the lock-up and quite a few had bloody noses.

'You really missed a good night lady,' the manager informs me as I check in.

My room is air-conditioned thus saving me from the gigantic mosquitoes for which Roebourne is famous. Alexander Forrest the explorer wrote of them in 1879: 'They are positively something dreadful . . . they stand erect until filled with blood, when they generally drop dead. Their sting is very sharp . . . if they get worse I don't know what I'll do.'

Roebourne has become a dormitory town, along with Cossack, Wickham and Karratha for men working in the iron ore industry. The towns are all in the process of being restored for the tourist industry as there are many fine old stone buildings such as the customs house, court house and church. The Withnell family were the pioneers of the district and there are monuments in their honour. One of Roebourne's most famous buildings is the gaol built by prison labour, mostly Aborigines working out their sentences. It is the main lock-up for prisoners throughout the Pilbara.

Ten kilometres away is Wickham, resurrected and rebuilt as a dormitory town for workers of the Robe River Mining Company. Right out on the end of the peninsula is a delightful little cove at Point Samson with white sand and emerald waters and named for a member of the crew aboard the *Tien Tsin*, a survey ship at the turn of the century.

The two other mining towns I now have to choose from are Karratha and Dampier so I choose the nearest, Karratha, and a motel called Omar's which has low rates they tell me. Other places in Karratha are very expensive as most people work on the 'Burrup', the peninsula where Woodside Petroleum is extracting liquid petroleum gas for export; the pay is higher than average.

Next day's coach lets me off at Omar's and disappears from sight before I can change my mind and get on board again to try somewhere else. It is not a real motel but rather a workers' camp of row upon row of demountables, or mobile cabins, communal ablutions block and workers' dining room or mess hall. At $25 a night without food it's not all that cheap and the next morning I realise I must move because as well as being less than pleasant it is in the industrial section of Karratha and 10 kilometres from the main town so travel anywhere requires a taxi. It's surprising that conditions for workers are so ugly in this multi-million dollar industry. Gregor McQuie, back in Kununurra, made the comment that this country needs slaves to run properly. These camps are upgraded slave quarters. There is nothing to soften the eye or soothe the spirit. There are caravans here with women and children living in them. To work here and live in such conditions must be worse than living in city slums where at least there is a large community to choose friends from and bright lights and entertainments. A few of the women I see look as dejected as the Aboriginal women I'd seen back in Roebourne, waiting outside the pub for their men to finish drinking.

In areas or towns where there is no public transport the help of the tourist bureau is essential so I search it out in the large Karratha Shoppingtown which has arcades, Woolworths, Coles and a Super K-Mart and a preponderance of young people with two or three small children in tow. In fact there are children everywhere, all well dressed and not whiney like city kids. The mothers don't look strained like city mothers so maybe it follows through. Only people with jobs live here and as the wages are good everyone is happy. Thinking back to my comments about Omar's I realise that the people living there are probably the ones who don't have permanent work and are itinerant workers passing through for seasonal jobs.

A lively and attractive girl called Lisé Maragliotta, whose marvellous name comes from a Spanish Egyptian mother and Sicilian father, attends to me at Jet Set Tours and sets me right about a few things I had been unable to solve further north. I move to the Walkabout Hotel while Lisé makes enquiries about tours for me.

Walkabout is a recently built hotel in Pilbara station style in keeping with Karratha, which was originally a cattle property and taken over when the miners Hammersley and Woodside needed space for expansion. It has an unusual architectural style of inner courtyards planted with palm trees and looks as though there should be horses tied to hitching posts. Fully booked! This is a shock as no way can I contemplate another night at Omar's. I beg for a broom cupboard if all else fails and they tentatively offer me a room they can't possibly rent because it has no television. I'll take it!

'You do understand though? There is no TV!' I assure the receptionist that I am prepared to rough it and spend a night without the flickering shadows. It's been done before.

That settled I dash back to Lisé to see what she has been able to organise. I am a traveller without my own transport and this makes sightseeing in the Pilbara just about impossible. Not many of the beautiful places in Australia have been so busy going about their own business that they haven't had time to throw their hat into the ring of the booming tourist industry. But this is true of the Pilbara at the moment. It's all there with its Wittenoom Gorge, the Burrup Peninsula, the Hammersley Iron Project, the Monte Bellos, but unless you are in your own vehicle it's very hard to see them. There are tours but they tend to be for people with lots of time to spare.

The Pilbara is spectacular with its stunning beaches, ghost towns, dramatic gorges, national parks and its fascinating historical background of pearling and goldrushes and all of this in a year-round perfect climate. Back at Jet Set I learn that there are free tours available to the Dampier Solar Evaporated Salt Mine Lookout, the Hammersley Iron Project and the onshore facilities of Woodside Petroleum. The catch, however, is that in order to participate you must be in Dampier which is a $25 taxi ride each way from Karratha. Clever Lisé comes to the rescue by phoning the public relations lady at Woodside and explaining my predicament.

'It's all fixed. Tomorrow morning at 9.00 a.m. the bus will collect you from your hotel and you can go on then to where they pick up the other passengers at Dampier. Then off you go to the Burrup.'

I am very pleased and stand ready outside the hotel half an hour before time just in case they are early. The mini-bus fills up at Dampier and we set off for the Burrup. Mandy is our tour leader and explains the project to us in simple language.

'Before we set off I'd like to say that we have a security regulation and you must not take photographs inside the actual construction area. All employees undergo a security test which takes five hours and also instruction in fire fighting, safety and environmental aspects.'

The North West Shelf Project is the largest resource development so far undertaken in Australia and the participants involved are Woodside, BHP, Shell, BP, Chevron, Mitsui and Mitsubishi. Gas from the project is already being used in Carnarvon, Geraldton, Perth and Bunbury and by 1989 the gas will be exported by ship to energy-hungry Japan where it will earn Australia export income greater than all other export income combined.

One hundred and thirty-five kilometres out to sea is the most spectacular part of the operation but unfortunately this is beyond our range of vision. This is North Rankin A, the drilling platform which is 214 metres from the sea bed to the top of the drilling tower, standing taller than a fifty-storey building. It is home to 120 production workers who work shifts two weeks on and two weeks off and are flown directly to Perth for their breaks. A fleet of helicopters acts as a bridge between the platform and the Karratha airport.

Tankers specially built to carry the LPG to Japan are the biggest ships in the world and so high that they would not be able to pass beneath Sydney's Harbour Bridge. Special tugs are needed to guide them in high wind conditions.

Not too far away on the other side of King Bay we can see the Hammersley Iron loaders and Dampier salt. This huge port on Mermaid Sound will soon rival anything else in Australia. In 1990 the ports will be handed over to the Dampier Port Authority to control as at the moment they are all privately owned.

On all sides the hills are covered with red rocks overpainted in grey and Mandy explains that this is caused by the high iron ore content. The whole area is like a gigantic quarry with little or no soil for the dried yellow grass seeking purchase in this barren landscape. It has an awesome beauty set as it is against the blue waters of Mermaid Sound.

The Burrup Peninsula is rich in archaeological sites: there are many Aboriginal rock engravings, shell middens and stone artefacts. Harry Butler is advisor to Woodside Petroleum on environmental issues and the Western Australian Museum carried out surveys prior to construction. Where possible important sites were fenced off and marked with red flags.

In the introduction to the Woodside publication *Do Your Bit for Burrup*, Harry Butler says, 'there need not be conflict between development and conservation; industry does not have to destroy the existing environment; enough thought, enough care, and planning based on enough knowledge and we can have our cake and eat it too . . .'

Leaving the construction site with its gargantuan cranes, pipes and holding tanks, the latter being in fact in-ground giant 'Eskies' for holding the frozen gas prior to shipment, we are taken on a tour of Hearson Village, temporary accommodation for the several thousand workers employed on the project. It is a short-term facility and there are no children and no domestic pets. It has two open air cinemas and two wet canteens, a fully floodlit grassed oval, gymnasium and indoor cricket facilities. Also a basketball court and Olympic-size swimming pool.

We are shown an excellent video on the history of the project, learning for example, that LNG (liquefied natural gas) is produced by refrigerating gas to a temperature of −161° Celsius. The super-cooled gas condenses to form a liquid occupying only 1/600 of its gaseous form. It is shipped in this liquid form and on arrival in Japan will be warmed to return to its natural state for use as a domestic and industrial fuel. A giant dredge, the *Leonardo da Vinci*, is currently gouging a channel for the tankers. Over and above the extraordinary fevered activity taking place is the astonishing affirmation that the project is on schedule and the first shipment of gas will roll at the end of 1989 as planned.

The popular swimming beach on the Burrup is Hearson Cove named for a man who tried unsuccessfully to grow cotton on the peninsula. Unloading horses he accidentally shot himself in the leg and when the wound turned septic he died. At the Cove, as well as elsewhere on the peninsula, exotic plants are forbidden for environmental protection reasons.

John and Emma Withnell with their eleven children were the pioneers of the area and Withnel Bay, where the main plant is being built, is named for them. Their main holding was at Roebourne but they journeyed all over the Pilbara coast and the saga of their first twenty-eight years of endeavour without relief is one of the great Australian stories of endurance in the early days of settlement. Emma Withnell, the 'Mother of the North West', with two children and one 'on the way', came ashore at Cape Lambert, the other side of the bay from the Burrup after a dreadful storm which took most of their supplies including boots. Walking on burning sand caused them all much distress until they were able to make wooden clogs and sheepskin wraparounds. Undeterred Emma followed her husband in their search for better land and five months later gave birth to a son. Isolation was their chief handicap added to primitive living conditions and the yearly threat of cyclones. Emma stood her ground, however, giving birth to all eleven children without medical help, educating them herself and living to the age of eighty-six in full mental alertness until the end.

The North West Shelf Gas Project bears comparison with Emma Withnell for its pioneering zeal and relentless determination to gain its objective. May it gain from her example.

Tour over, driver Terry Coffey delivers the other passengers back to their cars in Dampier and takes me on to Karratha. It was an excellent tour and he tells me he used to drive buses all over South America for the London-based Adventure Safaris. He went to all countries in South America except Argentina but rates his experience here on the North West Shelf as equally exciting. He says industrial relations are very good on the project and there is a degree of loyalty among the workers he hasn't noticed elsewhere engendered by their pride in the project itself. I believe this because I now feel a pride in it myself and once again am astonished at how little is known about Western Australian developments in the eastern states.

Back to Karratha I have five hours to fill in before travelling on south at 8.00 p.m. so I decide to check on the Karratha Public Library. Once again I'm in a dilemma as the library is way out of town and a $7.50 taxi ride each way. It turns out to be well-spent money as the library is excellent. As part of some reading dug out for me by the librarian I come across an interesting passage from a book by Jennie Hardie called *Norwesters of the Pilbara Breed.* It concerns the Aboriginal strike over wages in 1946. Among the sixty people arrested was Don McLeod, who has been in the news recently for 'kidnapping' drunk Aborigines and taking them to a faraway place to 'dry out'; Aboriginal people appear to be in favour of his actions. McLeod was born in 1908 in Meekatharra and educated at a Stella Maris school which he says made him anti-authoritarian. For three years he was a member of the Communist Party. He comments:

> The blackfellows treaded lightly on their uncultivated land, which they managed since time began, limiting their numbers to what the country could safely carry. They kept the country fresh and green for the benefit of posterity. In 150 brief years, we, the white people have nearly ripped the guts out of it. Who were the best citizens?

The Woodside publication *Do Your Bit for Burrup* is an attempt to try to prevent the huge gas project from 'ripping the guts out' of the Pilbara.

12

SHARK BAY, DENHAM, PEARLERS, CHRISTIANS, LIVING FOSSILS, DOLPHINS AND DINNER PLATES

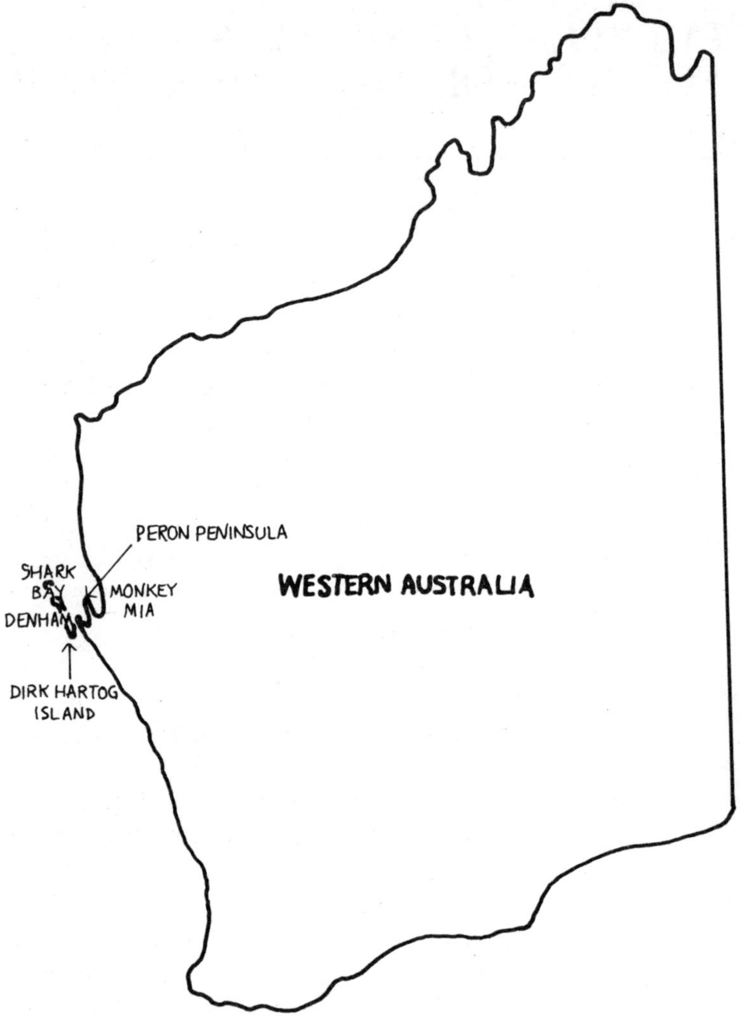
PERON PENINSULA
SHARK BAY
MONKEY MIA
DENHAM
WESTERN AUSTRALIA
DIRK HARTOG ISLAND

My seat companion on the overnight coach to the Overlander, a nine-hour journey, is a young lad called Martin who is returning to boarding school in Perth after spending the holidays with his parents at Hearson Village on the Burrup. His dad is a mining engineer and he has lived in Kenya, Nigeria, Tanzania, Burma, Thailand, the United Kingdom and Singapore. His whole family say the Burrup is the best place they've ever been.

We arrive at the Overlander, a roadhouse alone in the wilderness and I check out the accommodation in case the minibus to Shark Bay does not come this day and I have to spend twenty-four hours here. There are cabins available but thankfully the minibus does arrive at about 9.00 a.m. and the driver/owner Noel agrees to take me through to Denham, a two-hour drive. I am the only passenger and I hear on the way how he and his wife, Liz, got sick and tired of the city and came to Denham to enjoy life and are doing so to the full with the minibus service plus a little general store to keep them in touch with the human race. The country we drive through is red soil with small pale green shrubby tress dotted about with the eternal saltbush and spinifex. Emus dart about, then suddenly before us on the road is a huge one with a cluster of chicks about his great splay feet. Noel says it's a 'he' because the male is the baby sitter in the emu family system.

We pull up and the father cocks a disdainful irritated head towards us and then with great dignity ushers his brood to the side of the road, most unwillingly. One baby is left behind so I jump out to pick it up. I really only wanted to look but father leaps to the protection of his offspring like an Exocet rocket. His long thrusting neck comes at me at the speed of light, just missing me by centimetres as I hastily put the baby back down on the road. It could have been a nasty accident as emu beaks are as sharp as razors and the thrust of the long powerful neck is lethal. Noel drives off apologising for not warning me.

In Shark Bay I find my paradise. I have called other places paradise: little islands in the West Indies, places in the Pacific, Indonesian mountain hideaways and lakes in New Zealand. But Denham, on Shark Bay, is very hard to define. It is beautiful to look at with its pearl-shell road, white sand, the sea green where it meets the shore and blue further out. But it is more than that. The climate is balmy, with a gentle cool sea breeze crisply taking the edge from the hot sunshine, and the people are real. They have time. They look at you and they talk quietly. I am somewhere else.

They seem to be saying, 'Would you like a cup of tea? Just sit down and relax. There's nothing to worry about. Just take it easy. Everything is all right.'

They offer me tea, Liz and Noel and their partners Brian and Mary. All four came here for reasons other than settling but found it so beguiling that they stayed on. It seems as though they are mesmerised and live in a dream. I am transported.

At their suggestion I decide to take a tent at the caravan park which is right on the beach and part of the Campus Holiday complex with communal showers but what a far cry from Omar's at Karratha! Pretty gardens on all sides and flowering trees and the white sand beach only metres away. The tent has zip-up mosquito-screened windows on all sides and beds for four people. There is a mini-fridge, a gas stove, all crockery and culinary utensils, a table with six chairs and a beach umbrella for outside use. Sheets and blankets are also provided. A practical paradise! On top of that the cost is a mere $15 per day so of course I will stay forever.

Nearby is a supermarket so I buy what I think is necessary for my first meal in paradise. Home-cooked food at last; every mouthful is delicious. Putting everything away I settle down to read about Shark Bay and its history.

The first European known to visit the region was Dirk Hartog in 1616 aboard his ship, the *Eendracht*. *Eendracht* is the Dutch word for 'concord' and early maps show the area as the 'Land of Concord'. We know that Dirk came ashore at Shark Bay because he took a plank of wood from his ship and burying one end in the ground, nailed to it one of his pewter dinner plates. Engraved on it were the names of some of his ship's officers and the date. Translated it reads as follows:

> The 25th October is here arrived the ship Eendracht of Amsterdam the Upper Merchant Gilles Miebas of Liege, Scipper Dirk Harticks of Amsterdam. The 27th ditto we sailed from Bantum, the Undermerchant Jan Stins, the Uppersteersman Pieter Doones of Brielle. Anno 1616.

Eighty years later in 1697, another Dutchman, Willem de Vlamingh, landed in Shark Bay and discovered the plate lying on the ground beside the rotted plank. He took it back for safe-keeping to the Dutch East Indies, leaving in its place another plate detailing his find and adding his own descriptive notes. The original Hartog plate remained in Java for a hundred years until finally being taken to Holland in 1799 where is was housed in the Royal Cabinet of Curiosities later to become the Rijksmuseum.

Two years after Vlamingh, in 1699, the English buccaneer William Dampier chanced by and gave the name Shark Bay because of the great number of sharks in the area. He described it as the 'fishiest' place he had seen so far and detailed the delicious meals of turtle, shark and shellfish enjoyed by the crew. He made no mention of the plate, however, and its next sighting was by the Frenchman Baron Jacques Felix Emmanuel Hamelin, a member of Nicholas Baudin's party exploring the Bay in 1801. He rediscovered the Vlamingh Plate on Inscription Point, Dirk Hartog Island, and replaced the post which had rotted away like its predecessor.

Seventeen years later, in 1818, yet another Frenchman, the explorer Freycinet under the auspices of the restored Bourbon regime, entered Shark Bay and dropped anchor 10 kilometres off Dirk Hartog Island.

Freycinet's first act on landing was to remove the Vlamingh plate and take it back on board his ship. His reasoning was that it was too dangerous to leave it in such an exposed position where it might be damaged by irresponsible people. He took it back to France for safe-keeping where it remained lost for over a century.

The chief purpose of Freycinet's expedition was to make a scientific study of man, his physical condition, physical qualities, ages, illnesses, domestic life styles, clothing, habitation, furniture, utensils and moral outlook. It was a significant anthropological expedition. He also smuggled his wife aboard and she later wrote a delightful account of the voyage.

The ship's company were in agreement that the Aborigines of Shark Bay were perhaps 'the saddest creatures in creation'. They appeared to live on shellfish and have the intriguing ability of being able to survive without water. At least this is how it appeared to the Frenchmen who were unable to find fresh water in the area. In order to scientifically prove the point the botanist Arago pretended to drink a glass of water taken from the sea in front of a group of Aborigines and, noting their lack of interest or surprise at such a strange act, concluded that for them it was normal to drink salt water. There is no record available to indicate if the Aborigines came to the conclusion that the Frenchmen were a strange species of humanity who drank salt water.

In 1940 the Vlamingh plate was rediscovered in France and in 1947 presented by France to the Australian government. It is now in the Perth Museum along with a replica of the Dirk Hartog plate. A replica of the Vlamingh plate can be seen at Point Inscription.

An interesting postscript to the curious story of the impaled dinner plates comes as part of Australia's Bicentennial celebrations when the Dirk Hartog plate was loaned back to the government which had been lobbying for its return for over twenty years. Naturally the Dutch feel it is important for their own historical artefact collection but as a gesture have allowed it to go on a journey around Australia, on loan to the travelling Shipwreck Exhibition. On its journey it will be protected by bullet-proof glass and an envelope of argon gas. Thus ends the story of the travelling dinner plates.

Fish still abound in the bay, snapper being the most sought after. Big signs are placed along beaches asking fishermen to report any tagged fish they catch as part of a survey on their proliferation. Protected from heavy Indian Ocean swells by reefs and sandbanks, Shark Bay is an ideal spawning ground for many varieties of fish. The nursery conditions likewise attract larger fish on the lookout for food and so the chain of bigger fish eating smaller ones continues culminating in enormous schools of predatory sharks sometimes numbering in the hundreds.

At the far end of the bay is Hamelin Pool, isolated from the main bay by sand spits and bars and having too high a concentration of salt to allow any life to thrive save the most primitive and adaptable. It is here that the stromatolites are found. These curious forms of life are living fossils of stones and more abundant at Hamelin Pool than anywhere else on earth. They are formed by the activities of micro-organisms, mainly bacteria, which form mats of gelatinous, slimy film which traps particles of sediment. The balance is critical as stromatolites will only form when the micro-organisms grow slightly faster than the sediment is deposited. Each day the organisms force their way upwards through the deposited sediment and so form a new mat to receive the next delivery of matter.

Stromatolites come in various shapes and sizes depending on the tidal currents and form elongated ridges up to 20 centimetres high or sometimes club-shaped columns or large domes. For a reason not yet perfectly understood the ridge structures always form up perpendicular to the beach. Stromatolites are of great scientific interest in determining the age of rocks because of the layers of sediment they hold.

Layers indicate when life evolved in the growth of the rocks. The oldest rocks in Australia which contain stromatolites thus indicating that some sort of life had evolved there are 3.45 million years old and found east of Port Hedland at Marble Bar. The algae which formed these old stromatolites are long since dead but the structures they helped to create remain preserved in the rock.

Stromatolites are not beautiful to behold and are very difficult to photograph as they look like nothing more than dirty brownish-grey rocks; my attempts to photograph them are to prove a complete failure. Their ability to endure fills one with a sense of wonder as they have been forming somewhere on earth since life began and continue to form in much the same way today.

A man I meet on my second day in Denham promises to take me to see Inscription Point and the stromatolites. His name is Arthur Bassett and this is his story.

Arthur, who has only one eye due to a spider bite years ago, lives in the pearler's cottage he was born in, hard on the white shell beach road that rims the small town of Denham. The aspect is south-west and away to the right is the distant outline of Dirk Hartog Island. The Useless Loop Saltworks are on the mainland opposite, conducted by a private company. The salt mined is not table salt but industrial, and dimly discernible on the horizon are several white pyramid shapes of stored salt awaiting shipment to Japan. The pyramids are on an island linked to the mainland by a causeway and it is from here that the giant salt tankers load the salt to take it north.

Arthur was born in Denham to a family who came to Shark Bay in 1883 as pearlers. Denham was the first pearling centre to start in the West and Arthur's ancestors were part of that endeavour. His grandmother landed at a place now called Monkey Mia which in those days was known as Eastern Bluff. The population then was about a thousand, including a number of Chinese. Shark Bay pearling was all done in shallow water, never more than 2 fathoms at the most. There were no divers in Shark Bay.

'We used dredges, towing six behind a lugger and they scooped the shell up. It was very hard work because it was all pulled up by hand. In the summer time here you get very low tides and the land can be dry right out to where those boats are anchored. You can walk around on dry land for up to five hours and pick up shell. Shark Bay shell is a smaller type than Broome shell because here, we are at the southern extremity of the pearling. Shell is about the size of a saucer with very nice little pearls. The shell was our living and the pearls were the cream. Plastic buttons were the end of the pearling industry.

'A big volume of shell went out from here but there was also a great wastage of shell because we only picked the best. If shell had yellow or blue marks on it, it was thrown away. We sold through Dalgety's, most of it going to Hamburg. A Jew with a lot of money would buy all the shell and then it would be distributed among the Jewish people. They all had these little metal punches at home and would stamp the buttons out at night time.

'My old grandfather, Captain Sunter had a windjammer and my grandmother's family opened the first free store in Launceston. She was born in Launceston in about 1850. The old grandfather traded between Scotland and Tasmania in the beginning and then later he came round to the West and traded from Fremantle north up to the China coast and Russia. He took the first load of stock up the West Australian coast and landed them at a place called Billygoat Hill near Cossack. My grandmother travelled with him on the boat and all her children, bar my mother, were born on the China coast. When the grandfather began to get too old for such trips they decided to settle in WA. Pearling had already begun in Shark Bay so he sold the windjammer in Perth and came up here as a pearler.

'My father's people were the early settlers of Roebourne. They opened the first hotel there. My father came down to

Dirk Hartog Island as a horse breaker in 1917 and my mother had a house on the island as well as the one here. Everything was done by lease and everyone leased their own ground or their own part of the sea. Just like leasing land for a farm. You looked after your own land. You cultivated your shell. You killed off all the starfish and generally worked your land. This is what kept Shark Bay pearling going. Dad met mum over on Dirk Hartog and when mum's brother died he moved over here and left the horse breaking to go into pearling.'

Arthur went on to describe lovingly the wonders of Dirk Hartog Island which is a grazing property today, owned by Sir Thomas Wardell and visited mainly by net fishermen who work around its coasts. According to Arthur it has enchanting coral reefs seldom seen by humans and lovely beaches only now being discovered and sometimes desecrated by thoughtless tourists in speedboats.

Arthur went to sea when he was thirteen on the luggers and was a skipper at seventeen. He went on to skipper trawlers as well as luggers, north as far as Roebourne and south to Fremantle.

'I found a lot of pearls myself but in particular a beautiful golden pearl which I had made into a ring for my wife.' He shows me the pearl the like of which I have never seen in my life. It is larger than a fat pea and glows with a golden translucent light as though lit from within. I ask him what caused the phenomenon.

'The shell has a golden tint to it and the secretion used to make the pearl is the same as that used to make the shell. The gold is in the secretion. We found this one ourselves but I can tell you, you open a lot of shells before you find a pearl. How many? Thousands maybe. You can sit down and open shells all day and not get a pearl and then another day go out and get one in the first shell you pick up.'

In the old days the pearling luggers would be out all week returning on Friday afternoons bringing a full cargo of shell with them. In front of each house, including this one, was a big shed and the bagged shells would be brought to the sheds for working. Each boat would have about sixty bags. The leases were held all over Shark Bay, right around to Monkey Mia, Dirk Hartog Island and the point. On Saturday morning all the shells would be tipped out into the sheds and then on Monday they would start to open them. The Bassetts had three shell openers and Arthur's mum was one of them, assisted by two Aboriginal women. Three or four others worked in the shed to clean up and bag the shell.

'Having such a big quantity to open they used to let them die first as they were easier to open then. There was a smell alright, just depending on how good your nose was. They didn't look for pearls while they were opening but just scraped all the flesh out into tins and then put it into big barrels called 'pogie pots' where it rotted for three months. Then it was boiled and the pearls went to the bottom. The liquid on top was bailed off. That's when you got the pearls. The boiling didn't affect the pearls.'

It was only the little bit of flesh from the shell that was actually boiled and I ask Arthur if it is edible.

'It is indeed. We use it a lot, curried. We tried to market it but the government said it had too much cadmium in it. Well, I disagreed with that because I've eaten it all my life. We've eaten it all our lives except the son who never eats it. They did a cadmium test on us and we all came out the same. The son who never eats it had the same level as the rest of us.'

The population of Denham is about 450 which includes old pearling families of Malay and Chinese stock. Arthur's son is a professional fisherman and the whole family are shell collectors. All of them dive with the exception of Arthur who had his lungs damaged years ago by coming up too fast. He has to go on an oxygen machine every two to three hours. There is still plenty of pearl shell in the bay but no market for it. Plans are on the way, however, for the production of cultivated pearls, as in Broome.

'They are kicking off north of Monkey Mia at a place called Rose. [Cape Rose was named for Rose Freycinet who accompanied her husband, the French captain of the *Uranie* in 1818.] All the shell will be strung on lines and have these little starters made of plastic inserted by biologists.'

Arthur has no time for bureaucracy and spoke disparagingly about instructions which came from Perth disallowing the dredging for shell on the grounds that it was destructive to the natural growth.

'You ask any old pearler and he'll tell you that the way we cultivated our ground by dredging was like ploughing a field and getting better growth by keeping it clean and weeding out the pests. The beds here got better and better with the way they were farmed and that's what kept Shark Bay going for up to sixty years. Pearling ended with the Second World War and now it is mainly fishing. Whiting, bream, mullet and schnapper.'

I ask Arthur for an explanation of the name Monkey Mia: 'As I said when my grandmother came here it was called Eastern Bluff and then a man called Stross came in on a schooner and he had a little monkey. He anchored in there a lot and so it became Monkey Mia, or Monkey's home. There used to be a big blackfeller settlement near there and *mia* is Aboriginal for 'home'. They lived well with plenty of wild life and fish and emu eggs and goannas and echidnas. But they've all died out now. Mixed in with the other races and disappeared.'

According to Arthur the latest petitions on behalf of the conservationists to have the whole of Shark Bay designated a national park will sound the death knell to the fishermen of the bay including his son. The 'greenies' claim that fishing disturbs the dolphins and the dugong but according to Arthur this is rubbish. He says the dolphin come in such profuse numbers because of the fish and spend whole days circling the fishing boats waiting for titbits to be thrown to them. And the dugong, he declares, are in their thousands and quite safe although he agrees that in the past the dugong were killed for eating. He claims to be a conservationist himself but believes that anyone who kills a fish or a bird or a four-legged animal for his own eating, is no danger to the natural order of things.

'It's the idiot with the gun who goes and shoots for fun who does the damage. There is a fine now of $400 if you catch a turtle. And yet other professional fishermen are allowed to go up the coast and catch turtles on their way to lay eggs on the beach. It's all wrong. There is no scarcity of dugong or turtles or dolphins here in Shark Bay. The biggest danger here is from the introduced animals like cats and foxes. If they put a bounty on them it would do a lot more for our wild life. Foxes are thick here. They eat the turtle eggs. And the Poms brought them in for sport! To chase and kill them! Foxes kill off all the small wildlife like goannas and little marsupials. We've got a big selection of lizards here and echidnas and many many birds. There is also the bustard or wild turkey. Emus and kangaroos and wallabies and wild goats. Goats can be quite destructive. But I'm a conservationist myself and I believe animals like kangaroos should be culled. Before we came here it was done by themselves according to the amount of water available and the numbers kept at reasonable limits. But now with the dams and stations there is water everywhere so they breed out of all proportion to their natural habitat.'

Arthur is a world-renowned shell collector and does most of his overseas shell business by mail. For several years after he gave up diving he travelled all over Western Australia for the Education Department giving lectures to children on shells and shell collecting. His answer to my query on the immense quantities of a tiny white shell found everywhere around the coast of Shark Bay was to define it as *Cardium hamelini*. Shark Bay is the only place in the world where it is found so profusely as it can only live in conditions of very high salt density in the sea. It could not live around Denham for instance. All the shell used on the road was brought here from the inner loops of the Bay where the wee crustacean proliferates. He explains the habitat:

'From the open ocean back into where they are, in Hamelin Pool, it's about 60 miles. You've got a 6-knot tide. It runs in for six hours so that ocean water comes in for 30 miles and then flows out again. The water that has been lying inland comes about 30 miles and then goes back, leaving a sort of buffer zone in between the two. It means that the water right back at the top evaporates and is not renewed and purified by the ocean water. It just runs backwards and forwards on itself, so that, plus evaporation, means the salt density is very high. Shark Bay has many inlets with the tide running in and out like this all the time. Little *Cardium hamelini* proliferates here. They have something similar in Argentina but it's not the same.'

The tiny pearl-white crustacean, about the size of a small watermelon seed, was named for the French explorer, Admiral Hamelin of pewter dinner plate fame. His name is also perpetuated in Hamelin Pool, one of the broad estuaries of Shark Bay.

According to Arthur there are over a thousand wild goats roaming the Peron Peninsula and he invites me to join a goat hunt along with his son, his granddaughter and another young couple. I ask why they want to catch a goat.

'To eat of course! I told you before that we don't kill anything unless we're going to eat it. What we don't eat ourselves we give to the dogs. Goat is good eating in a curry.'

Next morning I go round to Arthur's house after breakfast and we all pile into the van and travel east to the Shelly Beach area near Hamelin Pool with the smart goat-spotter dog sitting up front on the lookout. We drive for an hour or so through red earth spinifex country, oddly beautiful in a defiant, survivalist, waterless way. Always the same colour patterns of pale apple-green against red with the blue sky above. Arthur talks of an old Aboriginal settlement he found up the far end of the peninsula some time ago, littered with artefacts and having burial places and middens. He wrote to the Department of Land and Environment in Perth and back came a letter: 'Don't touch anything! Tell us exactly where it is. And do not go there again. Please mark the site on this map.'

It doesn't do for bureaucrats to send letters like that to people like Arthur. He did answer the letter, however, saying he couldn't remember where the site was and that he was in fact illiterate. Someone else was writing this letter for him and he couldn't read maps.

As well as his shell collection Arthur also has over a hundred birds. Each year he has to tell the department how many. One year he was one bird out on his count and they wanted to know why. He replied that he didn't know bird deaths were notifiable and that next time he would send the bird in a specially made coffin for interment in Perth by the authorities.

We cruise along the beach of tightly packed *Cardium hamelini*, 3 metres deep they tell me, and suddenly the dog sees his prey. Doors are flung open and the two young men and the dog race off in pursuit while Arthur gives instructions to Ina, me and granddaughter Kathy.

'You girls are the runners and it's your job to see that the goat doesn't come back this way. Just jump and shout if you see him coming and fend him off. Don't get close though. I think he's a billy and they've got big horns.'

Kathy, aged about four, is the most excited and stands, hands on hips and legs braced, quite ready to bar passage to the great goat whom I can now see is several times her size.

With the help of the dog the two men run the goat to ground and grabbing his horns throw him over on his back, bulldogging style. They then tie his legs together and bring him back to the van, flinging him into the trailer at the rear.

I get a good look at him and am glad I didn't have to fend him off as a runner. His horns are 30 centimetres long with a wicked little curl in them and he looks as though he has been master of the beach for a long time.

Just near where we are parked Arthur draws my attention to some prickly shrubs called *karara*. They look quite inedible but he says they served well as camel food in the old days. There is also a straggly, uninteresting looking tree about 2 metres high which is the famous sandalwood with its fragrant oil, so beloved of the Buddhists of Asia. Fortunately for the inhabitants of Shark Bay, Western Australian sandalwood, discovered in 1836, did not rival the more exquisite South Sea Island variety in the Pacific and so the people here were spared the ravages of the sandalwood trade and its bloody history of rape and destruction.

Over lunch Arthur talks of his childhood and how every weekend he went out with his Aboriginal friends who taught him how to live off the land. His inborn sense of conservation stems from these childhood experiences and is the fruit of his own experience. Until he was about ten years old the only access to Denham was by boat. Supply ships came by about every three months and people stocked up on what was unavailable in their own district. When the first dirt road was put in somewhere in the early 1930s everyone in the bay came to cheer the appearance of the brave car making the christening run of almost five hours from the Carnarvon road. It was the first time some of the locals had seen a four-wheeled type of transport and many of them laughed aloud at its strange appearance.

In the afternoon I take a walk along the main street past the hotel, made of *Cardium hamelini* bricks and the Old Pearlers Restaurant made of the same. At the top of the hill is the church, also built of shell and I learn that it is a communal church available for the use of any denomination. Inside there is much use of shell as decoration and the font itself is a large fluted shell of palest pink.

Catty-corner from the church is a curious ranch-style building half hidden by trees and having about it a faintly South

American look. I peer through the bushes trying to read some of the signs when a man speaks behind me.

'Are you looking for someone?'

'Not really. I was wondering if this was a hotel?'

'A hotel? Yes. It is indeed a hotel. It's God's hotel. My name is Tim Hargreaves. Please come in and meet my wife.'

These surprisingly warm and friendly people not only invite me into their house but also share their meal and their life story with me. Tim and Maggie built the house themselves from piśe mud-brick in the Spanish style with sleeping, living and kitchen wings set around an internal courtyard. It is all cool and green, warmed with great flowing shawls of purple and pink bougainvillea. The view of the blue and white village of Denham far below, framed by wide windows around the kitchen walls, is like living Delft ware, set in dark red blocks of piśe. From this height, the village and bay are more of a dream than ever.

Like so many others in Denham the Hargreaves had come for a visit and stayed for a life. They built and ran the Old Pearlers Restaurant down on the beachfront and later built the very beautiful rambling house here on the heights. Tim told me their story.

Both are British public school educated, Maggie growing up in a high-ranking army family in India and Tim at an Anglican boarding school with matins in the morning and evensong at night.

'I went out into the world with a great curiosity and called myself an agnostic. For ten years I roamed the face of the earth, at sea, as a hobo, as a searcher and then on a return trip to England met Maggie and married her within twenty-four hours. We came to Denham and began to build our empire. I got a job and on wages restored an old house that was on this site and also built and started the Old Pearlers Restaurant down in Denham. Children were coming along now and everything looked great. We had a beautiful little daughter and a son and I had a good job. Then all of a sudden the rug was pulled out from under our feet.

'Fire devastated our home and my daughter was inside. She was burned to death. Screams. I couldn't get in. Calling me. I was broken.

'Well as you know, when one thing goes wrong, everything goes wrong. I had insurance but there was none. Bodgy company. I'm in my late thirties and trying to start again as a penniless immigrant. And the death of my daughter. It broke me. You know what it is when you're depressed. You think of pulling the pin. Drinking. No peace. Angry and hostile with God. Then I got caught up with born again believers. They didn't look the other way or pass by on the other side of the street. I was skipper of a tug up north and I didn't like it much. I wasn't very good at it and I had a lot of close shaves. I used to pray to God but that's easy. The distant dad. But it wasn't good enough. I knew I had to find the personal God. I had to accept Christ as my personal Saviour.'

Tim went on to say how he and his wife became born again Christians and not only recovered from the grief of their lost daughter but rid themselves of the sorrow and pain, knowing she was now safe and happy. They resurrected the church, opening it to all denominations and made sure the door was always open. They rebuilt their house on the ashes of the old and worked forcefully for the God they now believed in so wholeheartedly. Tim says there are two kinds of Christians: those who accept the miraculous and those who don't. They have a chair in their book-lined medieval sitting room in which they say they have seen miracles occur. People cured of asthma, arthritis, pain and other infirmities.

I ask if pilgrims come to him for help and he says yes, sometimes, but more often by accident, as I had come today. All religions, all colours and nationalities, all faiths.

I ask him if Buddhists come.

'No. That is heathendom. Before I would never have used that word but now I do. You have been in those countries. You have seen the dirt and poverty and the pain and the misery. And who are the only people who do anything to help? The Christians. Of whatever denomination. Be it Salvos, Seventh Day Adventists (who upset the calendar a bit!) or even the Jehovahs. Like Mother Teresa in Calcutta they go in there and help the poor and the suffering and the weak.'

The intensity of Tim and Maggie's belief leaves a lasting impression on me allied as it is to their hospitality and good fellowship. They give me, as a parting gift, a copy of the New Testament in paraphrase entitled *The Greatest is Love.*

Monkey Mia is on the opposite side of the Peron Peninsula from Denham and a half-hour journey by minibus. We pass the golf course and the airport and the great gypsum clay pans from which gyprock plaster is made. The road runs through the centre of one, then on, undulating over low hills of saltbush and spinifex until blue appears on the horizon and we sweep down onto the wide expanse of beach that is Monkey Mia.

Large signs greet us warning that dolphins are animals and that special care must be taken on greeting them. They may be fed fish and patted along their flanks but on no account should they be touched near the breathing hole on the top of their head. Dolphins belong to the whale family and the ones that frequent Monkey Mia are called bottlenose dolphins. This type of dolphin can be seen performing tricks in aquariums all over the world but what makes the Shark Bay dolphins so special is that they are the only ones in the world which come in close to the shore in numbers of up to ten and mix freely with humans, allowing themselves to be patted and cuddled, apparently enjoying every moment of the close contact.

There is only one swimming inshore when I arrive and I learn that his name is Holey-Fin because of the wounds on his dorsal fin, probably from fights long ago. Before I leave there are six swimming in and out of the knee-deep visitors' legs and none of us is willing to leave until they do. Suddenly, with a flip of their tails, they turn seawards and are gone.

Since 1982 an American team of marine biologists has been living in the caravan park and studying the dolphins for ten months out of the twelve. The scientists follow them in runabouts and say that sometimes they see the dolphins travelling at over 50 kilometres per hour. Their life span is up to forty years and like man, they have a very large brain in relation to their body size. They seem to want to be friends with us and communicate with us. While I had been wading through the shallows to get a good photo, one creature saw what I was trying to do and came right up to me. Turning on its side, half out of the water, it flung its head back in what was nothing less than a Marilyn Monroe gesture and smiled. It was a real Hollywood smile, with perfectly neat white teeth gleaming and pink gums and long pink tongue. I could hardly press the button for laughing.

They swim like us, moving their tails up and down and not sideways like fish, and they prefer to breathe about every twenty-five seconds though they can hold their breath for periods much longer than that. When they give birth they are attended by a midwife and on delivery the newborn is taken to the surface immediately to breathe air. The mother and other females play a very important part in their upbringing and offspring stay with their mothers for three or more years.

Tearing myself away from the company of these endearing creatures I walk up to the ranger station to gather more information. There are three rangers on duty, two women and a man and I speak with Tony Bassolae. He got the job from the CES in Carnarvon and hasn't looked back since.

'We have five rangers here and our main job is to educate people on how to meet the dolphins. Although the dolphins are in control of their own situation they will retaliate if people touch them incorrectly. Being wild animals their only form of defence if they feel threatened is to bite or give the person a good whack with their tail. There have been several cases here that have needed to be treated with stitches after a go in with a dolphin. I've been hit by a dolphin tail myself and it left a really big bruise. There are seven dolphins which come in and will let you feed and touch them and some strangers that don't come regularly but will allow you to feed them. We recognise them from their specific markings and for the bits and pieces missing. They all have names. There's Holey-Fin and her two daughters Nicky and Holly. There are three males, Bee-Bee, Snub-Nose and Sickle-Fin. And another female called Puck. You can't differentiate the sexes by looking at them so we only know what we've been told by the researchers. They inspect their genitals which are all contained internally and examinable only through natural slits in their body.'

I ask Tony why the dolphins come in here and he says he feels sure it's primarily for the fish and secondly for the companionship of humans. He says dolphins are lazy and will take free fish anytime in preference to hunting it themselves. Other authorities have remarked on this apparent laziness saying that the phenomenon of dolphins rounding up fish and herding them into fishermen's nets is not really to help the fishermen but a wily way of getting easily for themselves the exhausted fish which struggle free from the net and so are easy to swallow up headfirst without too much exertion.

'Dolphins are very temperamental. Sometimes they come in for the fish and don't want to be touched; sometimes they don't even want the fish but just swim around keeping at a good distance. Sometimes they act as if everyone is their friend. We can pick their moods but it's hard for visitors to do that. Sometimes they come in just plain cranky and it doesn't matter where you touch them they'll have a go at you.'

I ask about their relationship with sharks.

'That's a tricky one. This is Shark Bay and there are plenty of them around. There are many different stories about shark–dolphin relationships. One old fisherman says he's seen them swimming together. Others say they've seen dolphins attack sharks and yet sharks have been caught with dolphins in their stomachs. If all these stories are true it leads us to think that perhaps because of the masses of fish in the bay the two do at least tolerate each other.

'Research here has shown that the males are dominant and that the gestation period is twelve months. I read everything there is about dolphins now that I work here. The more I'm here the more I know that the public need educating about the animals and how to treat them. They seem to like women and children but are always wary of men. Maybe it's something to do with memories of the past when sailors ate them.

'In the old days it was all bush here and fishermen came in to empty their nets, tossing the rubbish bits back into the sea as they cleaned the fish. An elderly couple, called Watts I think, used to come up here to fish and anchored their boat off Monkey Mia. Old Nin, the lady, got up one night and saw this dolphin alongside the boat so she tossed him a fish. The next night he was back again and this time put his mouth right up to her and took a fish from her hand. They named him Old Charlie and he became a regular visitor. That was in the sixties. The next stage was when a young girl coaxed him right in to the beach and gave him fish from the water's edge. Now of course there are many more that come in. We get about 36 000 people a year now to look at them and the dolphins never miss a day. Fully reliable. There are seven regulars but we have names for thirty. They aren't tagged because they are easy enough to identify, like humans. No two dorsal fins are alike on dolphins.'

Dick Smith (*Australian Geographic*, No. 7) has the last word: 'Wouldn't it be wonderful if we could see more places like Monkey Mia, where wild creatures that roam the vast oceans come inshore seeking human contact of their own free will? I'm sure that then there would no longer be any reason to feel uneasy.'

13

FAREWELL TO PARADISE, WILDFLOWERS, PERTH, MIRACULOUS FLOW OF WATER AND GOLD GALORE

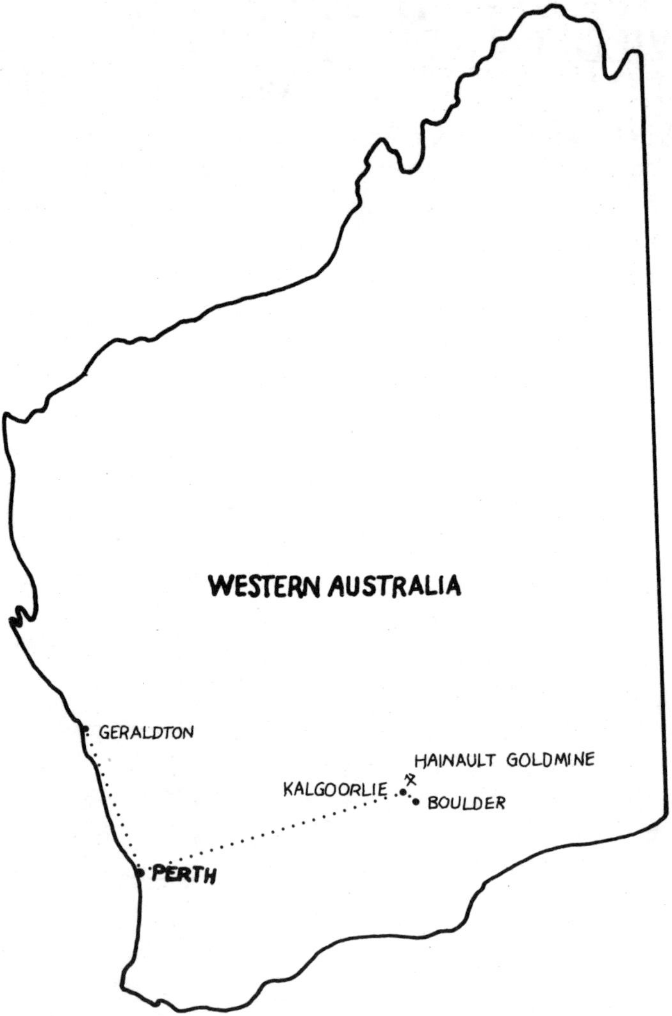
WESTERN AUSTRALIA
GERALDTON
HAINAULT GOLDMINE
KALGOORLIE
BOULDER
PERTH

That evening, my last in Shark Bay, I am determined to photograph the setting sun on the sandhills; the sunrays will be the last to hit the continent of Australia until tomorrow when the new day will begin with the first rays hitting Mount Warning behind Mullumbimby in northern New South Wales, where my brother lives. Shark Bay is the most westerly part of Australia and it is a memorable experience to sit here on the sand with gulls weaving overhead and see the great golden orb sink into the sea leaving our vast continent under a blanket of darkness and rest.

That night, going to bed in paradise for the last time I set my alarm for 2.15 a.m., ready for the early minibus to the Overlander back in the real world of the Northwest Highway. My Ansett connection to Perth is due at 7.00 a.m. so it is important to catch it and not be forced to spend twenty-four hours in the desert waiting for the next one a day later.

It is dark all the way out of paradise and I am glad. It hurts enough to know I am leaving, without having to be visually aware of it as well.

The coach arrives, on time as usual, and we set off on the ten-hour journey to Perth soon leaving the desert behind and sweeping down the coast towards Geraldton through a landscape stitched all over like a tapestry with Western Australia's fabulous wildflowers. People have told me I will only be seeing the tail-end of them but what I see is enough to make my heart leap. These flowers of the wilderness are not the colour of other flowers. They are brighter and richer and more profuse and more outrageously generous than any wild display I have seen before. Here on the Geraldton road they are strewn along our path like a multi-coloured carpet laid out for the advent of kings. The varying shades of red, blue, purple and yellow seem almost infinite in number as pinks in delicate clusters nudge their way through carpets of yellow-eyed daisies and are swallowed by clumps of purple and gold. The season is short and I am lucky to see this last loving flash of fire.

Stop at Cataby, the second worst roadhouse after Three Ways, and finally roll in to beautiful young, fresh, clean Perth at dusk. I have no time this schedule to visit the exciting city so I stay at the Criterion Hotel handy to the coach terminal and set off again the next morning for Kalgoorlie. The coach radio tells us it is Cliff Richard's birthday, the deathday of King Harold on a field in Kent and the day Eisenhower was born. Most memorable visual is a farm at Clackline with all its fences made entirely of piled up old tyres. Coach captain Peter is full of jokes.

'Query to Mae West: *How do you keep your youth?*

Mae West: *I send him a cheque once a month.*'

We stop at Merredin which gets the Smelly Toilets Award. A large pipeline has been travelling along beside us for some time now. Every few kilometres there are what appear to be valves or stop-cocks and small pipes leading away at right angles. This is the famous water pipeline which runs the 600 kilometres from Mundaring Weir near Perth to Kalgoorlie.

In the early days of goldmining in Western Australia lack of water was the biggest problem. There was enough water in rock pools and soaks for the Aboriginal people who knew the terrain but not for the hordes of goldminers, horses and camels which invaded the area once the 'rush' began. Each man required at least one gallon per day and horses twenty, so with up to 500 men and 100 horses on the field the local supply was soon exhausted. Water was distilled from brackish water drawn from bores but when the miners' numbers swelled to over 5000 the situation became desperate. The biggest distillation plant was at Coolgardie and in 1894, 100 000 gallons a day was distilled but the water was expensive and cost miners 2/6 a day plus one pound a day for horses and camels. Many men and animals died from drinking bad water and in 1896 the Government announced a mind-boggling plan to pump water nearly 600 kilometres from Perth. The cost in those days was even more staggering being estimated at 2.5 million pounds. Western Australia's population was a mere 110 000 so in the face of protest the government borrowed the money from overseas, authorised by an act of parliament.

Public opinion raged for and against the proposal and one prominent MP said, 'It has never been done in the history of the world and it never will be done'.

But it was done and became one of the engineering wonders of the world. The Mundaring Weir was built first and then came the difficult part. The goldfields were not only 600 kilometres from the weir but some 400 metres higher. To overcome this problem a succession of reservoirs was built, each one 120 metres above the last and so the water level was raised eight times before reaching its destination. This explained the valves I had noticed as we passed by in the coach.

The chief engineer was a man called C. Y. O'Connor who had already made his mark by building Fremantle Harbour in the face of Cassandra-like opposition and had organised the Western Australian railways so that they ran at a profit. It was due to his brilliance and scrupulous attention to detail that the pipeline was a success. Tragically, only a few months before the line was completed he took his own life, bowed down by the constant criticism and opposition to his gargantuan plan.

In January 1903, the water reached Kalgoorlie and the pipeline was officially opened to the applause of thousands and in a temperature of 41°C. The execution was faultless and the cost per gallon an incredibly low 0.06 pence at the reservoir or 0.10 pence delivered. In spite of this small levy on the populace enough profit was made to repay the loan in twenty-five years.

Since those days the pipeline has been improved and extended to outlying towns and villages and reached Norseman in 1936. The original iron pipeline has been replaced with modern welded concrete and carries an annual throughput of 16 million kilolitres. It services 100 towns and

2.5 million hectares of farms. The water takes two weeks to travel from Mundaring to Kalgoorlie and travels at half the walking speed of man, that is, at about 2.5 kilometres per hour.

C. Y. O'Connor is one of the great unsung heroes of Australia. Paddy Hannan, who found the first gold nugget in Kalgoorlie, certainly peeped into Pandora's box but without the genius of O'Connor it would all have been in vain. You can't drink gold.

We arrive in Kalgoorlie (from *kulgooluh*, Aboriginal for 'silky pear') just before four in the afternoon to find that the city is completely booked out due to the opening of the International Mining Expo. Not even a broom cupboard left, they tell me. Flashing my emergency letter from a travel industry friend I have the good fortune to have it read by the tourist information officer manager who knew my friend from old Singapore days. Taking pity on me he makes a few phone calls and offers me billet accommodation with a retired mining family. Couldn't be better. I accept the offer with delight and whisk off in a taxi to meet my hosts, Kath and Arthur Wright. The house is comfortable and lacks nothing in the way of televisions, videos, heavy duty washing machine and even a Solahart to heat the miraculous fresh water made available by C. Y. O'Connor.

The Hainault Goldmine, a tourist attraction where gold is also mined commercially, is my first excursion. My group of six all don hard hats and are crammed into a lift (just like miners) which is to take us 60 metres underground. It is an eerie feeling to drop so suddenly to such a depth. It is pointed out to us that there is a ladder running down the inside of the shaft in case the winder breaks down. Small comfort but good safety procedure. The miners actually working the operation are much lower at over 300 metres.

Our tour leader, Noel, a young man studying to be a mining engineer, gives us a very good show including turning out the lights to let us see how the miners actually work below ground by the light of a torch only. He shows us a primitive blaster known as the 'widow maker' because of its inefficiency. Blasting is strictly controlled now and permitted only twice a day at specified times. Many miners were killed by their mates indiscriminately blasting in the old days. I ask about the name 'Hainault' and although no one is sure it is suggested it is possibly an acronym for the initial letters of the eight original investors' names.

Later I ride the Rattler around the Golden Mile in Boulder, twin city to Kalgoorlie. A huge schistose lode was discovered here in 1893 by Canadian prospector Larry Cammileri. It was rich in free gold (initially over 5 ounces to the ton) and lower down even richer in gold telluride ore discovered in 1896. The lode covered 2.5 square kilometres and now has over 800 kilometres of workings down to 1300 metres. It is still being worked and so far has produced over 1200 tonnes of gold!

The Rattler Loop is run by the Railway Society and I am sold my ticket by an authentically dressed stationmaster, who happens to be a Maori from Te Kuiti in New Zealand. A tourist attraction today, the Rattler of the 1890s was reputed to be the busiest and best-paying line in the colony, hauling up to thirty-three passenger and goods trains in a day. The locomotives were 'N' class and known affectionately as 'Nellies'. Before we set off on our journey across the Golden Mile our guide gives us instructions on how to behave if we should see any Aborigines.

'Please don't look at them or call out to them or try to photograph them. They may retaliate by throwing stones at the train and we don't want to be responsible for broken windows.'

Shades of Ayers Rock all over again so we all sit firmly on our seats and fail to respond with so much as a flicker of an eyebrow when we pass a family group of Aborigines camped along the railway track, all having a jolly time and waving to us as we go by. I determine to disobey the regulations and at least give a polite responsive wave if we see them again but when we return along that same track, they have gone. Only their empty cans and some plastic bags remain. How rude and unfriendly they must think us tourists.

After Kamballie we see the Hannans Star headframe which was erected in 1897 and had rich gold close to the surface. One lode was found only 20 metres from the surface and had ore for a width of about 1.8 metres. We rattle on past the slime dumps which are in fact gold-bearing rock crushed to a fine powder and treated for the extraction of gold. These tailings are now being reworked with modern methods yielding gold in larger quantities than ever.

From here on all is desolation. Ding Bat Flats and the remains of the once proud town of Trafalgar are all that remain of a town that once had a population of 4000. The overhead commentary informs us that billions and billions of dollars have been extracted from this wasteland and we wonder why some tiny percentage was not put back to beautify the ground that yielded such wealth to the already rich and powerful. But there is nothing of beauty anywhere to be seen. Just the endless slime dumps and the puzzled groups of Aborigines drinking their beer and wine among the trackside weeds and waving in vain to stolid, blank-faced white folk aboard the toy train. Miners are not noted for beautifying the landscape from which they extract their wealth. Conrad observed in *Heart of Darkness*:

> This devoted band, called itself the Eldorado Exploring Expedition and I believe they were sworn to secrecy. Their talk however, was the talk or sordid buccaneers: it was reckless without hardihood, greedy without audacity, cruel without courage; there was not an atom of foresight or serious intention in the whole batch of them and they did not seem to be aware that these things were wanted for the work of the world. To tear treasure out of the bowels of the land was their desire, with no more moral purpose in it than there is in burglars breaking into a safe.

Build Xanadu on Ding Bat Flats. Now there's a challenge to a tycoon seeking brownie points in heaven! Make

Kalgoorlie a city of fountains, gardens and boulevardes of flowering trees, where the desert blooms and enhances rather than disfigures nature. Ah, what a dream! People would come from all over the world to see the Golden City that could be Kalgoorlie. A cool and fragrant oasis in the midst of a harsh and unremitting land that takes its toll of those who come unprepared for suffering. A golden dream.

Calming down I visit the Goldfields War Museum in Boulder with its lists of young men who sprang to the colours in the Boer War, the First and Second World Wars, Korea and Vietnam. In a glass case I am surprised to come across the naval uniform of my host Arthur Wright, who was a petty officer in His Majesty's Royal Australian Navy.

Waiting for the bus home I see a perfect rainbow arc across the city ending dead centre in the middle of the Golden Mile. There *is* gold at the end of the rainbow.

That evening, with two other billetees, I go on a pub crawl in Kalgoorlie which is humming with all its international visitors. Several of the hotels are architectural masterpieces of Victorian elegance and wealth. Sweeping cedar staircases are lit by chandeliers and outside, Juliet balconies, turrets, towers and topknots decorate them with festive frivolities. Later we take a voyeuristic stroll along Hay Street, famous for its girls for sale. Dressed in a variety of costumes ranging from cowgirls to can-can dancers, they lounge in the doorways of their narrow cubicles looking provocative and enticing. There is a short queue at one closed doorway but the other half dozen are fresh out of customers in spite of the crush of mining engineers in town.

Herbert Hoover worked in Kalgoorlie as representative of the giant Conzinc Riotinto at the turn of the century. He had a poor opinion of Australians calling them 'the laziest, shabbiest people, totally without morals and ambition, that I have even seen'.

Kalgoorlie's most famous daughter is Eileen Joyce, the internationally renowned pianist. I could not find out anything about her from the tourist brochures. Kath and Arthur tell me she turned her back on Kalgoorlie when she became famous so now Kalgoorlie has turned its back on her.

From a brochure I learn that all the gold ever mined in the world amounts to about 100 000 tonnes and that 2000 of these tonnes were mined in the Kalgoorlie area; enough to fill two Olympic-sized swimming pools. While the Golden Mile is still producing, outlying mines, such as Kanowna, only 20 kilometres away have become ghost towns. Kanowna had a population of 12 000 at its peak of production in 1912 but the gold only lasted twenty years. In its heyday it had sixteen hotels, two breweries and many churches but now all that remains is rubble and a railway platform, the only recognisable sign of former human occupation. People say that at night it is thronged with ghostly travellers waiting for trains that will never come.

14

FOLLOWING EDWARD JOHN EYRE AND ADELAIDE'S MAD MASONS, DESERT OUTPOSTS, CAMELS, KANGAROOS AND WOMBATS

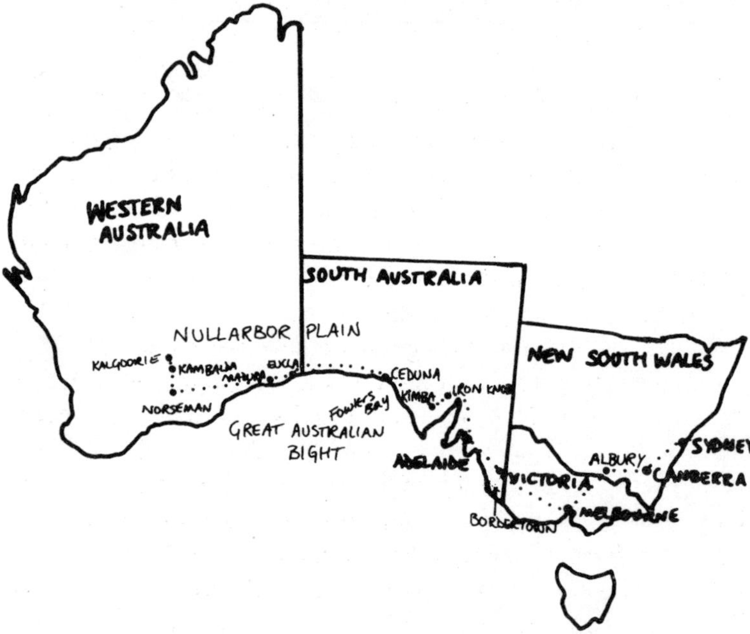
WESTERN AUSTRALIA
SOUTH AUSTRALIA
NEW SOUTH WALES
NULLARBOR PLAIN
KALGOORIE
KAMBALDA
NORSEMAN
EUCLA
CEDUNA
KIMBA
IRON KNOB
Fowlers Bay
GREAT AUSTRALIAN BIGHT
ADELAIDE
VICTORIA
BORDERTOWN
MELBOURNE
ALBURY
SYDNEY
CANBERRA

Next day it is time to travel south and east through the nickel town of Kambalda and on to make a lefthand turn at Norseman and across the Nullarbor Plain. The journey is to be 2770 kilometres to Adelaide and will take thirty-six hours. At 4.30 a.m. I spot a sign, 'Wombats, camels and kangaroos next 300 kms'.

Our captain, Arie van Wageningen, tells us to put our watches forward one and a half hours and passes around three books of photographs he has prepared himself and which show in detail the fauna, flora and minerals of the landscape we are now travelling through. Each page has distant and close-up shots of flowers all neatly labelled. Rosy dock, wild hops, wahlenbergia (bluebell), bluebush daisy, yellow groundsell, poached egg daisy, western myall, purple pimpernel, white western rosemary, purple love creeper, satiny bluebush and the many varieties of wild hibiscus. The names read like a poem and I guess at the reality of these flowering plants as we speed across the great flat plain of the desert.

After Balladonia and Caiguna we stop at Cocklebiddy and I remember that not far from here, on the cliff top of the Great Australian Bight, is a cairn marking the spot where the overseer Baxter was speared to death by Aborigines in 1839. Baxter was the companion of Edward John Eyre on the fateful journey of exploration to find an overland route across the continent from Adelaide to King George's Sound and Albany. After the death of Baxter and the loss of most of the stores Eyre continued on foot with one loyal Aboriginal guide, Wylie, and almost lost his life. The Eyre Highway is named for him as well as a peninsula, a small town, a mountain and a huge salt lake.

The coach slows down and comes to a halt, allowing a herd of twenty or thirty camels to cross. Where did they come from and what are they seeking so earnestly, loping along at a half-trot, eyes fixed on some distant goal beyond our imagining? They appear oblivious to the great bulk of our coach, giving it not a sideways glance as they pass over to disappear in a cloud of red dust towards the distant flat rim of the horizon.

Stops are at the desert outposts of Madura and Eucla, the set-down point for the old Telegraph Station, and on and on more desert hours to Yalata in the Aboriginal reserve of the same name. Some 200 kilometres north of here is Maralinga where the Aboriginal people became so innocently involved in the atomic tests held forty years ago. The food in the road-house isn't so good so I join a fellow passenger from the coach at the bar for a beer. It's 7.00 a.m. She's a pleasant Aboriginal woman who tells me she's been trying to get back to her home out of Alice Springs for about a year but can't seem to make it. She's been dropping in on relatives all the way from Perth and just gets held up each time.

'But I think I'll make it this time,' she says. 'I'm going right on to Adelaide and then straight up to Alice Springs.'

I toy with the idea of getting off here myself and going down to Fowlers Bay. The bus service isn't at the right time, however, and a taxi too expensive so I have to put the idea aside for the next time.

Fowlers Bay was the base camp from which Eyre set out on his epic journey and is reputed to be a pretty little place. Nearby also is Cape Nuytz and Nuytz Reefs named for Captain Peter Nuytz who sailed this way in his ship, the *Gulden Zeepard*, in 1627 and was the first European to see the southern coast of Australia.

We pass over the dog fence which is 1.5 metres high in places and runs an incredible 10 000 kilometres to keep dingoes away from sheep. It began last century as a simple fence around a property owned by Robert Bruce at Coondambo, 280 kilometres north-west of Adelaide to keep dingoes out of his property. With its introduction he was able to dispense with shepherds and the idea was eventually extended to enclose vast areas of South Australia.

In some places the fence is patrolled by boundary riders who make checks every fourteen days. Work is now in progress to replace the old wire with new plastic fencing which will drastically cut the maintenance costs. The fence caused a wombat explosion in the 1960s, particularly in the Fowlers Bay area, when it was estimated that more than 160 000 of the roly-poly tunnellers were in residence. As they were earth burrowers by nature the fence was no deterrent to them so an electric fence, powered by solar cells, was brought in to solve the problem.

At the very pretty coastal town of Ceduna my Aboriginal friend from Yalata waves me a cheery goodbye. She's not going to make Alice Springs this time and is going visiting again she says.

Our new captain is Dominick and he describes the mallee scrub to us with its saltbush and blue brush, tells us of the Jesus birds who walk on water wearing caps of red feathers and how Lake Eyre to the north is the lowest point on the Australian continent. Poor Eyre. Everything named after him seems to be the lowest, the driest, the most barren, the saltiest and the most hostile — except for this Eyre Highway which is a marvel.

Dominick now puts on for us the best and most appropriate video of my whole journey. It is his own private copy of *The First Four Billion Years*, produced by Dick Smith's *Australian Geographic Magazine*. It shows in magnificently drawn and photographed detail how this landscape through which we have been travelling came to be and all the changes and upheavals and times of drought and times of abundance it went through to bring us to this point in time. The plants and animals which adapted to its extraordinarily harsh conditions and either survived or passed into oblivion are depicted and the Aboriginal people who lived here and brought their own particular genius to bear in creating a way of life under conditions known nowhere else to mankind. I hope the video is shown wherever possible to people travelling through this still so misunderstood and little known land.

Iron Knob is breathtaking. It reaches up out of a bland domestic landscape like some great black giant emerging from the bowels of the earth. This is work. This is power. This is the mightiest in the mighty. Iron. Steel. Force. Energy. And wealth.

My travelling steam is beginning to run out and my intake valves are beginning to clog up as we roll on through Port Augusta, Port Pirie, Port Wakefield and finally into Adelaide. As with Perth I don't have time to explore the Festival city but spend one night in a very unusual hotel not far from the terminal.

The Earl of Zetland is part of what was originally the South Australian Freemasonry Complex on the corner of Flinders and Freeman Streets, now called Gawler Place. Records show that this is part of original town acre 233, first allotted to James Fisher in 1837 at a cost of twelve shillings. Thirty or more years later in 1869 it was taken over by the Freemasons and a Masonic hall erected here by the brethren. A time capsule was placed in the stone wall and laid over, in true Masonic tradition, with a mason's trowel. A photograph of the trowel now rests in a hallowed case in the Board Room.

The first licence for the Earl of Zetland was granted in 1870 to Thomas Bastard and the hotel name was chosen because the Earl of Zetland was Grand Master of England from 1844 to 1870. Bastard and his son were also lessees of the local swimming baths and Charles Bastard styled himself 'Professor of Natation'.

The heads of King Solomon and Hiram Abif were hand-carved keystones over the porchways in the original building and when the hotel was remodelled they were placed on pedestals and can now be seen in the Colonial Room.

Staying at the hotel is a journey backwards in time with comfortable bed and modern bathroom yet a strange eerie feeling in the corridors of goodly masons and their families dossing down here under the watchful eyes of their heroes, Solomon and Hiram.

The morning coach departs for Melbourne, and as we drive through the beautiful village of Hahndorf, settled by immigrant Germans in the 1870s, I see rain for the first time in four weeks. It is a dry continent.

This is *tatiara* country, the Aboriginal word for 'good'. It's hard to believe that the aforementioned Edward John Eyre was appointed Protector of the Aborigines in this area in order to save them from being murdered, poisoned and shot by early settlers who regarded them as vermin.

We stop in Bordertown, birthplace of Prime Minister Hawke, and see some albino kangaroos, and then on to the Wimmera. But this is all familiar scenery and a landscape I know. It's a world away and a quantum leap from that other part of the continent, the Outback, the Top End and the West.

Melbourne to stay with friends and then Sydney via Albury, Canberra and Yass and my great trek is at an end. Peter Porter, an expatriate Australian poet said, 'You are always closer by not standing still.'

Not standing still, but moving around this great land has brought me to a closer understanding of the incredible place I call my country. No longer the mythical Martian landscape devoid of people and living things but a kaleidoscope of wonder and high endeavour set with brave bold strokes on a canvas of colours all its own. Three colours are burned forever on my inward eye. The red of the earth, the apple-green of the low trees and the never-changing, relentless blue of the enormous arc of the sky.

BIBLIOGRAPHY

Brokensha, P. *The Pitjantjatjara and their Crafts*. Aboriginal Arts Board, Sydney, 1987.

Davidson, B. R., and Graham-Taylor, Susan. *Lessons from the Ord*. Policy Monographs, Centre for Independent Studies, St Leonards, Sydney, 1982.

Douglas, Malcolm. *Follow the Sun*. Rigby, Adelaide, 1978.

Durack, Mary. *Kings in Grass Castles*. Currey O'Neill, Melbourne, 1974.

Edwards, Hugh. *Port of Pearls*. Rigby, Adelaide, 1983.

Eyre, Edward J. *Journals of Expedition into Central Australia*. Boone, London, 1845.

Hardie, Jenny. *Norwesters of the Pilbara Breed*. Karratha Library, Western Australia.

Keneally, Thomas. *Outback*. Hodder and Stoughton, Sydney, 1983.

Lands, Merrilee. *Mayi*. Magabala Books, Broome, Western Australia, 1987.

Lockwood, Douglas. *The Front Door: Darwin 1869-1969*. Rigby, Adelaide, 1968.

Marchant, Leslie. *France Australie*. Artlook Books, Perth, 1982.

Phillips, Valmai. *Romance of Australian Lighthouses*. Rigby, Adelaide, 1977.

Powell, Alan. *Far Country*. Melbourne University Press, Melbourne, 1982.

Smith, Dick. *Australian Geographic*, No. 7, 1987.

Thomas, Athol. *Bulls and Boabs*. Rigby, Adelaide, 1977.

Walker, Roy. *Poems*. Argyle Station, Western Australia, 1986.

Walker, Roy. *Bush Ballads*. Argyle Station, Western Australia, 1986.

Webb, Martyn and Audrey. *Edge of Empire*. Artlook Books, Perth, 1983.

Wilson, H. H. *Cyclone Coasts*. Rigby, Adelaide, 1980.

Woodside Offshore Petroleum Pty Ltd. *Do Your Bit for Burrup*. Karratha, Western Australia.